Peace Beyond Understanding

Consoling One Another

Terence P. Curley

Emmaus Design
P. O. Box 889, Marblehead, MA.. 01945

Copyright © 2010 Terence Curley
All rights reserved.
ISBN: 1453891080
ISBN-13: 9781453891087

Other Titles by Terence P. Curley

Book Publications
Console One Another: A Guide to Christian Funerals
The Ministry of Consolation: A Parish Guide for Comforting the Bereaved
Healing the Broken-Hearted: Consoling the Grief-Stricken
A Way of the Cross for the Bereaved
Six Steps for Managing Loss: A Catholic Guide Through Grief
Healing: Questions and Answers for Those Who Mourn
The Ministry of Consolers
Planning The Catholic Funeral

Audio/Visuals
Journey to Healing: A Ministry for the Bereaved (DVD)
Through the Dark Valley: Healing Steps for Managing Grief (DVD)
From Darkness to Light (CD)
Arise and Walk: A Christian Grieving Guide, (DVD),
Finding Your Way Through Grief, (CD)

May the peace of God,
which is beyond understanding,
keep your hearts and minds
in the knowledge and love of God and of
his Son, Our Lord Jesus Christ.
Amen.

(Order of Christian Funerals 233)

In loving memory of my father Edmund & my mother Eileen Curley. May they enjoy the peace of the Kingdom of Heaven.

Contents:

Introduction		1
Chapter One	The Ritual's Call To Console	13
Chapter Two	Bringing Order To Funerals	31
Chapter Three	The Ritual's Symbols For Support	39
Chapter Four	Phases In Grief Ministry	55
Chapter Five	Selecting Scripture For Liturgies	67
Chapter Six	The Ritual's Biblical Roots	79
Chapter Seven	Children and Loss	97
Chapter Eight	The Church's Prayer for Healing and Hope	111
Chapter Nine	Prayers for Special Circumstances	121
Chapter Ten	Grief Ministry In the Parish	131
Chapter Eleven	Cremation and Bodily Resurrection	143
Chapter Twelve	St. Paul and the Ministry of Consolation	153
Selected Bibliography		163

Introduction

The "ministry of consolation" is a multifaceted experience of service in the Church. As a ministry, it serves a variety of intense needs facing community members while they struggle with separation and loss in life. This ministry has been with the gathering together of Christians from the very beginning. In order to appreciate this ministry, we must go to the twofold source of scripture and tradition. All pastoral care must be rooted in the way the presence of God is constantly being revealed to every generation. The salient aspects of this ministry take shape when we search the scriptures and what is known of Christianity's earliest times.

This book is a revised edition of my previous title, *Console One Another: A Guide to Christian Funerals*, published by Sheed & Ward in 1993. Since then, there have occurred changes and new insights concerning the burial of a Christian. In this edition, I have included pastoral insights along with an appreciation for the ritual's liturgical expressions. I hope that the reader who wants to participate in the ministry of consolation will be greatly assisted with these words. I consider this book to be a necessary companion for my recent title, *Planning The Catholic Funeral*. This expanded revised book elaborates on and explains the process of ministering to those who mourn in far greater detail, both for individual ministers and their respective parishes.

Theology of Death

Before we set out to explore the earliest origins of this ministry, we need to examine what was the driving influence for the ministry. This entails appreciating the theology of death. From the beginning, Christians participated in the life and remembrance of the Lord through saving signs, The noted Jesuit theologian Karl Rahner, in his treatment of the theology of death, tells us about the "Sacramental visible union between the Death of Christ and the Death of a Christian." Through visible signs and rites, we participate in the life of Christ. These visible signs represent how our very redemption is appropriated. This wonderful appropriation of Christ's death transforms our own. This is with us for our entire lives and energizes and graces our ministry of consolation.

Karl Rahner cites Baptism and the Eucharist, along with the Sacrament of the Sick. These three sacraments have clear reference to Christ's death and, consequently, our own way of ministering and facing our death.[1] Through signs and symbols, the inexpressible mystery of God is given to us.

Ministry and Identity

The theology of death and our ways of going through the experience of loss are linked. A better understanding of the scriptural references to the sacraments better prepares us for the liturgical and pastoral care of those who are suffering from grief.

Effective ministry requires that we connect our very selves to what we say and do. Our being present to others is

---

1 *On The Theology of Death,* Karl Rahner, Herder & Herder, N.Y., 1961, p.73

an intensely spiritual reality, which must be grounded in our own faith identity. In the ministry of consolation our anchor for action requires that we become increasingly mindful of our own baptism. Our prayer life and reflections have to include an awareness as to how we become visible signs to others.

The requirement to be a minister of care is first and foremost a realization that we are living out our baptismal commitment. As we have been washed or immersed in the waters of baptism, we have died and been buried with Christ. We must suffer with Christ so that we become glorified in Him. Our expectation for ministry must include suffering personally and with those whom we encounter. There is joy for the Christians who so very often must first join their suffering to the Lord's. Our own death must be confronted in the context of faith.

In the Eucharist there is the proclaiming of the death of the Lord. We must participate in Jesus' Passion if we are to rise with Him to new life. From the earliest moments, when Christians gathered together, especially at the death of a member, there was the singing of psalms and the remembrance of Jesus' presence.

The breaking of the bread celebrates that time until the Lord returns in glory. The bread of life is the gift of consolation given from the one who is the Shepherd of Paradise. It is in paradise that we live with refreshment, light, and peace.

The anointing of the sick is a visible sign of our need for healing and restoration, given with explanation in the fifth chapter of the Letter of James. "Pastoral Care of the Sick: Rites of Anointing and Viaticum" properly expresses the Christian journey toward the Kingdom. Keeping in mind that we are a "threshold people," we are in need of strength and consolation during our times of illness We need strength as we stand on the threshold to cross over into the Kingdom of God. The actual sacrament for the dying is Viaticum. It can be defined by two Latin words "via" which means way or journey and "tecum" which means with you. The Eucharist is the bread of life for the journey which we take with us when we cross over the waters of death, that threshold to eternal life. It is the food for the way.

Toward A Theology of Bereavement

The ministry of consolation acts as a catalyst for theological reflection and speculation regarding our personal and communal response to grief. Whenever there is loss in the believing community, there is a need for expression in faith-filled ways. Our laments must mirror our relationship with the Lord. This is an issue apparent for Christians from the very beginning.

The mourning practices of non-believers can distort the Christian's experience of death. Bereavement without the consideration of the context of faith is not in keeping with the Christian tradition. Paganism's perspective is totally different. The bereavement period of time developed from despair; It lacked the Christian emphasis upon light, deliverance, and rest.

Early Church writings emphasized that the souls of the deceased live on in the bosom of Abraham. Such an image brings healing and hope which enables us to form new relationships in faith with those who have died.

Signs and Symbols

A good amount of this book is concerned with signs and symbols, which play a vital role in the *Order of Christian Funerals* and in grief ministry. Christianity's early signs and symbols provide us with images of faith. In the primitive church, the funeral rituals relied on symbols of shepherds, fishermen, and banquets.

Early necropolises provide us with archeological evidence of the theology that emphasized the promise of eternal life. Early stories about Jesus in the New Testament, the stories from the Hebrew Scriptures, are artistic preservations that assist us in ways to find a theology of comfort and consolation.

We are provided with our belief as it is distinguished from the misled culture of the day. Through the telling and retelling of important passages from Jesus' ministry of healing, we are given a theology of hope. This study of soteriology (*soter*, from the Greek: to heal) is the necessary backdrop for the ministry of consolation down through the ages.

The present *Order of Christian Funerals* cannot be appreciated if it is viewed in a vacuum. It is connected with faith and theology down through time. Actually, according to historical perspective, the ritual for the death of a Christian did not begin with the funeral. Rather, it began with viaticum. This is when the Christian received the Eucharist for the last time before dying. There then followed a funeral service in the home. The service of the home not only prepared the deceased Christian's body for burial but, also, for the transfer to the church.

Liturgical Care for a Threshold People

Liturgical roles in celebrating funerals are very much a consideration of the ministry of consolation. In many ways the very purpose of this book is to illustrate how essential and connected the funeral is for grief ministry. The funeral does set the tone for the bereavement process.

The celebration of the liturgy is far more than merely assigning roles. It is the preparation, which is sensitive to the needs of those who will be participating in the ministry. Liturgical ministry is connected to pastoral care. We must always have pastoral commentaries for our rituals. If the only concern is with rubrics, considerable care will be lacking. We must become better aware of ourselves as a "threshold people" eagerly waiting the Lord's coming to fully establish the Kingdom of God. Our rituals are rites of passage for ourselves as a "pilgrim people of God." Through expressing our faith in ritual actions, we become more aware that we are on the threshold of the Kingdom of God. As our loved ones cross over this threshold, so, too, will we at the appointed time in our lives.

Ritual Moments and Ministry

The death of a Christian and the liturgical moments for ritualizing our losses has varied and developed in practice from the Church's earliest days. Initially, the care for those close to death was the moment or time for the Sacrament of the Sick. As we have already noted, Viaticum is the sacrament for the dying. These moments took place in the home. After the Christian died, there was the preparation and care of the body. This also took place in the home to prepare for being taken to the church. By taking the body to the church, the deceased Christian is seen as a follower of Christ connected to everlasting life.

In the sixth century, it was noted that the bishop prayed a thanksgiving for the deceased Christian's life, along with prayers for the forgiveness of sins. At the very end of the ritual there is the final kiss of peace. This is not a farewell but rather an expression of deep communion. Life in Christ knows no farewell.

Our present ritual cites various moments or stations for the celebration of prayers. While we have not included the anointing of the sick as the beginning of ritual moments, it must be included in the ministry of consolation. The rituals surrounding the death of a Christian can be likened to a final journey in faith. For deceased Christians, there is the gathering together of those who loved them in life and now pray for them in death. These moments have developed down through the ages to the present form in the *Order of Christian Funerals*. These moments have been called "stations" or "stops" along the way in the funeral journey. They are ministerial moments that may be appreciated in a variety of ways. Each moment brings healing, hope, and a way of assisting those who mourn to place their loss into the context of faith.

Family Liturgies

The early ritual moments or stations may be called "family liturgies." They are signs of concern for family members and those who were close to the deceased Christian. These prayers are offered as consolation at the critical time of loss. The family liturgies include: (1) Prayers After Death (O.C.F. 101-108), (2) Gathering Together in the Presence of the Body (O.C.F. 101-111), and (3) Transfer of the Body (O.C.F. 119-127). Further reference is given to these moments in this book. We will now briefly consider the "Family Liturgies" as they apply to our caring for one another.

The Family after the Death

This initial family ritual serves as a model for prayer at the first pastoral moment following the death. The funeral ritual tells us that we should be mindful of adaptations that may occur due to circumstances. The presence of the minister of consolation is meant to bring a calming effect (cf. OC.F. 102) This may well be the first contact the minister has with the family. If so, it is important to appreciate the circumstances in providing comfort and eventually in preparing the funeral.

According to pastoral psychology, this initial model is very much in keeping with "crisis intervention." The presence of the minister is an intervention that helps the bereaved to accept the loss.

It is necessary for ministers of consolation and all those who want to assist the bereaved to become familiar with this model in the ritual. Whether this takes place in the hospital, home, or funeral home, the prayer model communicates deep meaning and purpose. It consists of an invitation to pray, a scriptural reading, the Lord's Prayer, a prayer for the deceased, and a prayer for those who are grieving. It concludes with a blessing.

At the time of death there may well be chaos and possibly some disorientation among the mourners. The presence of a minister allows ministry to begin at this critical time It does not put off helping the bereaved place their loss into the context of faith. The very action of prayer calls forth the rich resources we have in faith. Amidst the numbness and disorientation there is an awareness that we are Christians who can and must call upon the name of the Lord.

Gathering Together

In the ritual there are specific prayers for gathering together for the first time in the presence of the deceased lying in death. **Gathering Together in the Presence of the Body** (*O.C.F.* par. 109-118) is a ritual that which shows reverence for the body. Again, from the point of view of pastoral psychology, we realize that there is a perspective that helps us better understand the acceptance of the loss. For those struggling with acceptance, viewing the body leads to initial acceptance that the death really did occur.

This second family liturgy is when the family first comes together either before or after the body has been prepared for burial. Again, the presence of the minister of consolation provides an atmosphere of "sensitive concern and confident faith" (*OCF* par.110)

Processions for the Family

The third family liturgy is called **Transfer of the Body** (O.C.F. 119-127). This occurs when the deceased Christian's body is transferred to the church or the place of committal. This part of the ritual highlights the aspects of journey. The procession is the carrying of the loved one to the church or the place of committal surrounded by family and friends. Usually, in the beginning of the Christian's life (infant baptism), we are carried, surrounded by family and friends, into the church to be baptized. Now, at the end of our earthly journey, we are once again surrounded by our family and friends, who carry us into the church. Now, our hope is to prayerfully send forth our loved one to the Kingdom of Heaven. The image of being a 'pilgrim people' is also fulfilled by processing in this manner.

People of the Watch

Since the beginning of the Church, Christians have watched and waited for the Lord. Our understanding of "vigil" has replaced the Anglo-Saxon word "wake." The meaning of "vigil" is of being awake or alert, watchful, sitting up with someone, staying awake.

The vigil is the first liturgical action of the Church. When this takes place in the parish church, we realize the ecclesial dimension of the Christian's life and death. The importance of celebrating the vigil in the church cannot be overestimated. I have found as a pastor that the experience of the parish outweighs any descriptions or suggestions. Once parishioners experienced being with their loved one in the familiar and holy environment of the parish church. In our age, funeral homes are constructing 'chapels,' which are gaining popularity in our secular society.

This practice happens when the elderly person does not provide for the place for the funeral to occur. If the remaining relatives do not participate in parish life, they choose an option foreign to their loved one's faith. On the other hand, it has become necessary for funerals to be celebrated in this way due to the fact that relatives planning the funeral are not practicing their faith. Fortunately, there is the provision in the ritual for the celebration of the funeral liturgy outside of Mass (see *Order of Christian Funerals* par.178). This is where the chapel is used. In some ways, the chapel does help the Church to reach out to those alienated or estranged as well, to experience the ritual and the Christian funeral. Many Christian funeral directors are to be commended for encouraging sacred rituals with families when they are making preparations for funerals. There are other circumstances as well (including disabilities/infirmities etc.) which merit the celebration of the funeral liturgy outside of Mass.

We as a Church have to foster the ministry of consolation, especially with our end of life rituals. These rituals are essential for our community's spirituality. They are also essential for the grieving process. They are not added on; rather, they are the very tone and theme at the death of a Christian that integrates the entire grieving process.

This book is intended to touch on many aspects of grief. Reference will be given to the *Order of Christian Funerals* throughout (note "OCF," is the abbreviation for references). Once again I want to mention that this is an expanded view since this work was first published as *Console One Another: A Guide to Christian Funerals,* by Sheed & Ward (1993). Later the work was distributed with Rowman & Littlefield. Now, almost twenty years later, with a variety of changes in our understanding of grief and liturgy, it is once again being published with the hope that it will be a continued reference for all those dedicated to care for the bereaved in the ministry of consolation.

Pastoral Action

It is not uncommon for anyone beginning this ministry to feel overwhelmed and very often without support. When we mention that we want to minister to the bereaved, people mistakenly say that we are preoccupied with death. That is far from the truth and the meaning of this ministry. This ministry of consolation is about life and we are very much ministering to those who need our help in processing and going through their time of sorrow with them. We are loving companions for those who are so very often confused and overwhelmed by grief. We have to teach those who are not knowledgeable about grief that this is a time through which we all have to go in our lives. We have to pray for guidance and provide that to those who need to be instructed about this ministry. Our prayer with them as we help them sort out their memories, dreams, and reflections about loss is that they will receive a peace beyond understanding. A peace that comes over us as we express our deepest feelings in ritual actions.

Chapter One

The Ritual's Call To Console

This chapter orients anyone wanting to minister to others during bereavement. It highlights the ritual's new rituals, which are very sensitive to needs facing the believing community during times of loss.

Grief touches everyone. This is an important observation for our culture, which denies the reality of loss. Separation and loss, especially due to the death of a loved one, is a difficult reality for any of us to deal with. Physicians, professional counselors, and even the clergy often recoil in the face of death. Suffering continues for those who are experiencing grief when the necessary help is not provided.

This book intends to assist those who are seeking ways to help manage the very real pain of separation and loss. It is written in light of the *Order Of Christian Funerals*. This Roman Catholic ritual for the burial of a Christian is very different from previous rituals. Those rituals were books explaining to the priest or deacon the mechanics of a sacrament, the gestures and actions to be performed to make the sacrament a sacrament. The *Order of Christian Funerals* was composed for the caring community. While it still gives the mechanics necessary it adds a whole new dimension: a call to the community to come together and care for the living. This ritual serves as a bridge between what is expressed in liturgies and what is done in the daily life of the parishioner.

There is an overarching pastoral goal for this book to help the bereaved and those who minister to place their grief into a wider religious context of meaning. This is no easy task. It doesn't happen overnight or by some platitude or formula.

Rather, it can happen with the commitment and care of the community. The community is called to respond in a helping way where our society has failed to assist the grief stricken. The community by truly being a community can help the bereaved remember the loss of a loved one in ways very different from our death denying culture. This chapter is meant to emphasize new ways to relate when people are grief stricken.

Called To Console One Another

The funeral liturgy is the beginning of the expression of grief. It is a painful and often shattering time for the grief stricken. The liturgy has to be appreciated as an important way of expressing the loss of a loved one. The way we ritualize can make a significant difference in the way a family grieves. It is a time to remember and pray for the deceased loved one. It is also a time to pray and assist the bereaved relatives and friends. The new liturgy is conscious of the needs of the living, left to express their loss.

When we think about the funeral it is important to put into perspective the whole grief experience. The funeral experience is a doorway for the bereaved. As such, that doorway can be a dark and forbidding one that drags a person down so that all that is experienced is an overwhelming, suffocating loss. On the other hand, that doorway can and should be a bright one leading the bereaved through to glimpse eternity's shining morning beyond the loss.

Paul Irion in his work on funerals and bereavement, provides us with a way of appreciating what the funeral does in the process of bereavement:

> The funeral itself is only one part, sometimes even a small part, in the whole psychological process of meeting bereavement. Yet, because of its public nature it is extremely important. It represents the response of the community or the church to the emotional experiences of the mourners. Thus, it cannot be regarded as either irrelevant or contradictory to the psychological process of acceptance, release, expression and assimilation that enable the mourners to endure and overcome the tremendous disorganization of his life which has taken place.[2]

Using the imagery of pilgrimage and Christians being a pilgrim people, the new ritual likens the funeral to a short journey of two or three days for the bereaved. Just as on a short journey, there are stops along the way, and these stops are called "stations" in the ritual. The stations represent times for a liturgical intervention into the personal grief. They become celebrations of the deceased's life and a reaffirmation of Christian life for the bereaved.

---

[2] Paul E. Irion, "The Funeral and the Bereaved," in *Resources for Ministry in Death and Dying*, ed. Larry Platt and Roger Branch (Nashville: Broadmann Press, 1989) 211.

These stations represent a time or times for the family to be in and of the community. The community, by being with the bereaved, is called to share in the healing power of Christ. The community is called to make this vital response for not only those who are gone, but especially for those left in the community.

Very often while we grieve, communities with their actual identities appear. We realize that there are very real human bonds that connect us to one another. Along with our emotional needs, certain physical tasks illustrate how communities respond to the call to console one another. It may entail cooking a meal for the bereaved and their families, who just received from a neighbor a ride from the airport from a neighbor. Or, it may mean babysitting or being with an elderly family member who otherwise would be alone during this time of loss. Sometimes, I have seen people very quietly give some financial help by slipping some much needed money to families. Parishes really come alive when everyone realizes and sees that they can often do something to help.

The vision of the new ritual is to relate the stations to the emotional needs of the bereaved. Ministry done by both priest and community during the time of the funeral will have far-reaching effects in the way grief will be done. True pastoral care can happen if the ministers of care embrace the real intentions that originate in the ritual.

It is important to experience the ritual as a resource for pastoral care. If it is allowed to degenerate into a book of directions or rubrics for the celebration of liturgical actions then the entire meaning in ministry will be lost. In keeping with the perspective of the new ritual being for the whole community, there is before all the liturgical stations a brief outline of the features in the rite. Highlighted are participation and ministry.

This is very much in keeping with the spirit and words of *Vatican II*. The role of the People of God as expressed in the *Constitution On The Church, Lumen Gentium,* is very clearly presented.

The descriptions of the Church from the Council document speaks to members as a pilgrim people. Not only are we pilgrims, but we are pilgrims traveling together, we are companions on the journey toward the Kingdom of God. Pastoral care is realizing that we share in the same journey. How we treat each other on the pilgrimage is of paramount importance. We cannot journey alone; we are connected and must cooperate. Just as any journey cannot be completed when everyone wants to go a different way, we cannot bypass our companions, but must bring them with us. We were baptized into a journeying people. This makes us all responsible for our brothers and sisters in the community.

The ritual stresses the importance for the parish leadership to emphasize that the community is responsible for the ministry of consolation or caring. This directive finds its roots in the Gospel. "Blessed are they who mourn; they shall be consoled" (Matthew 5:3). The parish leadership is called upon to make known to the parish: (1) the meaning of death, (2) the purpose and significance of the rites for the dead, and (3) information on how the parish community assists families in liturgical preparation.

The site of the community as primarily responsible for the care given to the bereaved is an important empowering reality for all to share in pastoral care. Care for the bereaved is not thought of as something left up to the clergy. It is not seen as something reserved as a special action in the community. There is now an including of the entire parish. This view of church is far more empathic and demonstrates the unity among all of the believers in the parish. The ritual very clearly instructs us:

> Members of the community should console the mourners with words of faith and support and with acts of kindness, for example, assisting them with some routine tasks of daily living. Such assistance may allow members of the family to devote time to planning the funeral rites with the priest and other ministers and may also give the family time for prayer and mutual comfort.

(Order Of Christian Funerals: par.10)

Resistance to change is still a fact of life in the post Vatican II Church. Just because something is promulgated does not mean it will necessarily be accepted. Much work is called for. Not only must the community be trained by the parish leadership, priests, and ministers, must confront the pain of death and the transforming nature of the new ritual.

Such demands call for new approaches in the training of parish ministers. These new approaches must not only allow for learning, they also must address the spiritual and feeling aspects of the new ritual. Empathy and the ability to walk through the minefield of raw emotions when death is being experienced draws deeply from spiritual wells that must be replenishable. I would suggest that parish leaderships become involved in a retreat that mirrors the new ritual. A three day retreat that follows the stations or moments in the funeral ritual also ought to allow for those on retreat to re-experience and learn anew from their own personal experiences of loss.

There is a need for the parish ministry to be prepared in the way they encounter the bereaved. Support and information for the parish staff and those who volunteer to minister is necessary. The difficulty of ministering to the bereaved can be appreciated in the following example:

Marian recently graduated from a prominent divinity school. She did very well in her academic work and easily found a position as a pastoral associate in a moderately large Roman Catholic parish. She was enthusiastic and hopeful about ministry. A call came from the local funeral director about a funeral. Suddenly, Marian became upset, knowing that she had to see the family. Her hands became sweaty, and she felt uncertain about how to talk with people in the funeral home. This was an aspect of ministry she really did not want to have any part of in her life.

There are probably many issues involved in Marian's response to meeting with the bereaved. There may well be some unresolved grief in her own life. There may also be the fact that she really hadn't thought out this aspect of ministry. Divinity schools and seminaries often provide academic ways to deal with the bereaved. The actual experience of communicating with the bereaved is something that is seen as 'on-the-job training."

In some respects, it is true that we learn and sharpen skills by doing ministry. Grief ministry, however, is an area where we need to prepare ourselves and realize that we can't do it by ourselves. It should be done as a community, where the caregiver interacts with others about his/her feelings in ministry. Ministering to the bereaved does not have to be approached with fear. It can be a rewarding ministry of love. The minister's presence does make a difference. Support and help from the parish community allows ministers to walk through the valley of darkness with the bereaved.

It is important to see the new ritual in the context of ministry. The ritual relates to critical grieving moments in the lives of the bereaved. The new prayers address these moments, both spiritually and emotionally. The prayers are for the bereaved and elicit an emotional response. They attempt to go beyond their route Sunday school prayers and praying we learned when we were very young. In this critical moment, they call us in a mature way to new responses to the Spirit at work. If we look at the prayers, keeping in mind what is happening emotionally with the bereaved, our approach to ministry will be more fruitful and satisfying, both emotionally and spiritually.

New Rites In The Ritual

There is an important addition to the revised rite, which illustrates how the rite acts as a bridge for the bereaved. The Related Rites and Prayers *(OCF,* paragraphs 98-127) are moments in pastoral care that may have far reaching effects in the lives of the bereaved. There are three parts in the funeral journey under the heading of Related Rites: (1) Prayers after Death, (2) Gathering in the Presence of the Body, and (3) The Transfer of the Body to the Church or to the Place of Committal. We have already considered certain aspects of these rites in the introduction. Now, let us further expand our understanding of the importance of these "ministerial moments" for communities of faith.

The related rites affect the parish community in an important way. This is an area where the laity is invited to minister to those suffering loss. These three stations have to be reflected on in order to ensure that a pastoral response is given by the community.

The stations should be the subject of pastoral instruction for the caregivers. They play a vital role in our appreciation of the lay ecclesial ministry. The baptized are called to participate and minister in special ways during these "stations." A sad commentary is when these rites are not provided. The challenge is to ensure that parishes, with their members, offer these significant ritual times.

The parishioner/caregiver represents the parish community. He/she is the person who can be the leader at the related rites. The reason for having the parishioner do this is not necessarily due to the advanced age or the present shortage of priests. It is an action empowered by baptism. The adult baptized Christian represents the believing community in moments of prayer. This once again highlights the role of the community as the primary pastoral caregiver. It fosters and cooperates with the belief that there are many ministries in the parish.

Critical Situations

Some knowledge of crisis situations is helpful for the pastoral caregiver, but developing a 'crisis style" is really a lifetime endeavor. The more we learn about responding rather than reacting, the more effective the caregiver will be in helping those experiencing a crisis. Eugene Kennedy, in his book on crisis for non-professional counselors, raises the question: "What can we do?" His description of the crisis in answer to the question helps in learning to respond:

> By its very nature, a critical situation is usually brief, that is, limited by time in some way or other. The goal is ordinarily straightforward: to get the individual functioning again This is different from trying to read hearts deeply or attempting to rebuild personalities. These objectives are common sense ones; their achievement depends on our understanding of them and our own possibilities and limitations. Nothing replaces a level head and good human instincts: These are the elements in the foundation of our response in any difficult circumstances.[3]

The parishioner-pastoral caregiver is a non-professional. The identity is that of being a member of the Christian community offering services. The operative word is 'offering.' It must always be kept in mind that people reacting to grief are not always ready to accept what is being offered.

The caregiver may be called to a hospital or home to offer prayers on behalf of the parish. This type of a situation requires awareness about the critical event. The parish has to establish a program of training for the caregiver who may offer prayers at the time of death.

The Prayers After Death (*Order Of Christian Funerals,* par. 104) provide the caregiver with a format or model for praying with the deceased family. This is an initial way to bring comfort

---

[3] Eugene Kennedy, *Crisis Counseling, The Essential Guide for Nonprofessional Counselors,* New York: Continuum Publishing Co., 1986)

to the bereaved. Some of the characteristics of the bereaved at this time should be in the mind of the caregiver.

Certain Grief Reactions

Certain grief reactions are greater than others, and there are different types of grief The sudden and unexpected death of a loved one creates a more intense reaction, whereas, when there is some anticipation, as is the case with a prolonged illness, the reaction may not be as intense.

The very intense type of grief is known as 'high grief." When the experience of loss is with someone with whom we don't have as significant a bond, then the loss may be considered a 'low grief" reaction.

Death is the severing of a bond or what is known as an effective tie in our lives. We know that in our familial and social sphere, we have many ties of greater and lesser degrees. It is important for the pastoral caregiver to be aware of the different relationships among the bereaved. Everything is not always as it first appears when the caregiver arrives.

The following example illustrates reactions: Marian arrived at the home of the deceased to be greeted by a middle aged man who appeared not to be too troubled. He explained that the deceased was quite elderly and had been sick for a short while. When Marian went into the parlor, she saw two younger women who were very tearful comforting an older woman. The women were the deceased's widow and his daughters. The middle-aged man was a son-in-law.

The initial reaction was to think that everyone would be very calm at the death of the older person. The opposite, however, is often the reality. It is important to realize that there are a variety of responses, but there is never a correct or incorrect response. A minister may well encounter people who seem to flip between low and high grief, depending on what is touching them emotionally at the time. We must always remember that when people grieve, they are not just grieving for the elderly parent who was fading before them. They are also grieving for that young parent who held them when they were small and hurt. Emotionally, a person, no matter what age, is once again the small, hurt child looking for the parent who is no longer there to offer comfort The most descriptive response to the loss of a loved one is that of shock. It is difficult to accept the fact that someone has died. This is all the more difficult with an accidental or sudden death. There is numbness and possibly some disorientation as to what has really happened.

The reaction to a sudden loss is described by one author as follows:

> Grief is preceded and complicated by a shock reaction when the loss occurs without any warning, e.g. as a result of accidental death. The shock reaction has two components: one is denial, "It can't be true." The other is a form of depersonalization, a state of emotional anesthesia, in which the bereaved feels numb or unreal or that the world is unreal. This condition is frequently described as "weird," "I feel like a zombie," "It is like living in a dream." In extreme cases, these symptoms are severe enough to immobilize the bereaved's movements and speech so that he appears to be mute and immobile. Frequently, the observer notes that the bereaved is dazed, walking slowly and talking with great difficulty.[4]

---

[4] H. Robert Blank, "Mourning," *Death and Bereavement,* ed. Austin H. Kutscher, Springfield, Ill., Charles C. Thomas Publisher, 1974, p. 205.

The pastoral caregiver is the person who illustrates that the death has in fact happened. Otherwise, the priest or parish representative would not be standing in the midst of the family with a book, ready to offer prayers. This is a difficult place for the caregiver to find him/herself. Yet this is the very place to be to bring about a ministry of love in a crisis. The presence is a healing presence for those who are suffering.

The prayers are to bring comfort to the bereaved and pray for the dead Christian. Comfort is really given when the prayers help the bereaved to accept the reality of death; they are the first expression of the family acting together after the loved one has died. Along with the spiritual strength, there is the psychological help in accepting what is very painful.

Crying and other expressions of loss while prayers are read are very acceptable. The liturgical action is meant to help release the emotions. The celebration of the prayers should continue even if there is considerable emotion expressed. Some caregivers may be shaken by such an occurrence It is understandable for the caregiver to feel upset by the anguish of others. What has to be understood is that the crying is a catharsis or a cleansing and is very important in the process of grieving. The letting go of a bond depends upon the expression of grief.

The Church has a very important role for the managing of grief. The prayers and symbolic gestures help from the very beginning to redefine the bereaved relationship with the deceased. This is one of the most important actions in what is known as grief work. Grief work is allowing ourselves to remember the loved one and accept the reality that one has died. It is a readjusting to a loss that makes us feel as if part of ourselves has died. Tears and symbolic actions have to happen for us to really accept such a loss.

The prayers at the time of death are not lengthy. The pattern consists of a reading from scripture, a response, a prayer, and a blessing. Alternate prayers are available for a lay person, a deacon, or a priest. The blessing may be a signing on the forehead of the deceased with the sign of the cross.

The words accompanying the signing ask God to allow the deceased Christian to rest in peace. This action is a farewell to the Christian to go forth as a pilgrim to the Kingdom of God.

It is significant to note that in the rite of baptism, the welcoming is done by the signing of the cross on the forehead of the infant. The family and friends participate in the signing of the cross. In the ritual of baptism, the new candidate for the sacrament is signed with the seal of salvation. The focus at the beginning of the Christian life is toward the journey's end.

The end of the earthly journey is brought home to the family and friends as they come together to pray for the person who just died. There is involvement by the family and the parish. These prayers may naturally follow from the Sacrament of the Sick when the person who was anointed passes to eternity. There is a unity between the sacrament of the Anointing of the Sick and the prayers in the ritual.

In the *Order Of Christian Funerals* emphasis is given to the importance of continuing a liturgical action when the person has died. The *Order* acknowledges that ministry must continue after the death. It is not the time for the minister to leave the stage because the sacramental action is done. This is very evident in critical situations.

Gathering in the Presence of Our Loved One's Body

Another new aspect of praying according to the ritual with the family is the Gathering in the Presence of the Body (*Order Of Christian Funerals* par. 109).

In the United States, there is the custom of the family arriving early to view the body before the wake. In the past, when wakes were longer, there was a custom to have the first night only for the family. That custom has gradually disappeared with the advent of wakes being moved out of the home and into funeral parlors. The new rite affirms the importance of this time alone with the body for the immediate family. This is the critical time for many family members most touched by the loss. Often it is the first time some have seen the loved one's body since death. For many it also represents the beginning of the two or three day gauntlet. It truly brings home the reality of the death.

At such a critical time, the presence of a community representative can have a healing effect. Here it is important that the family be aware of and consent to that presence beforehand. Before any prayers are offered, the family should have the option of a few minutes alone to gather in the presence.

After the time alone and before others arrive, a brief service is performed to not only engage the family in the process but to pray for God's healing presence throughout the funeral process. There is the sprinkling with holy water to recall baptism. The theme of the journey is consequently deepened. The family is encouraged to express themselves with the signing of the cross on the loved one's forehead. The participation in this way obviously gives the family a better sense of caring for their loved one in death. They are clearly participating in burying the deceased. Their feelings are affirmed and allowed to come forward.

Transfer of the Deceased Loved One

This station (*Order Of Christian Funerals,* par. 119) in the ritual is very emotional for the family. Time has stood still; the reality of the wake has been established. Now that reality must give way to the final separation of funeral and burial. It is very important in the bereavement process. The bereaved family has to let go of their relationship with the deceased, and the bond has to be reestablished in a different way with the deceased loved one. The prayers with the family are for strength. They also illustrate that the procession to the Kingdom continues and calls them to change.

The prayers for the transfer of the body are done before the body is removed to the parish church. This may be done prior to the funeral mass or at the vigil liturgical service during the last night of the wake. In the new ritual, there are options available for where the vigil service will take place. The family may decide that the church is more appropriate than the funeral parlor.

God's presence with us is expressed in the prayers as the family processes to the parish church. The Lord being with us in our coming and going is a consolation. The reading of Psalm 122 is an uplifting expression for the mourners. There is the going to the House of God to receive peace, a kind of peace the world cannot give.

The Necessity of Instruction

In many ways our society is not structured for those who grieve. Separation and loss are avoided and denied at all costs. This is especially true when we suffer the loss of a loved one in death. People may be concerned and offer condolences without the ability to appreciate the long term effects loss has on the grief stricken.

It is not uncommon for co-workers, friends, and even parishioners to shy away from the reality of loss. This makes good grief work all the more difficult for the bereaved. It also does not allow those who mourn to find peace and consolations from relationships that could help them heal.

Bereavement is a time of chaos and upheaval. It can lead us into darkness or bring us into a new and enlightened faith. The more aware we are of the spiritual and psychological aspects of grief, the better we can help others to live through their losses in meaningful ways. Our catechesis or instruction for the community is essential for good grief.

Catechesis reminds those who grieve that we live with the bright promise of immortality. Our society treats life as if it has ended. Our trust in God, however, teaches and informs us that ' life is not taken away; it is changed."

Pastoral Action

This chapter has addressed special additions to the ritual. Highlighted are the ways the community may participate in the healing ministry that our baptism invites us all to do. The ritual is very much a bridge for the expression of our emotions as whole persons. It also is a bridge connecting the believing community to the bereaved in new, healing ways. The ritual is a clear call to all the baptized to respond and participate in ministering to those among us who are suffering a loss. In our day and age, we need to not only be aware ourselves as to what it means to take the journey with the important times of stations for prayer, but also to teach others about this. The funeral hasn't to be something we do, not talk about. Rather, the more knowledge, the better for our spiritual appreciation of what it means to "have a funeral."

We live in a society that does not always realize the importance of ritualizing our losses. Our being in the community means that there are moments of evangelization both within the community and certainly with those outside of it. The funeral explanations we give can and do touch the lives of those who will go through the loss of a loved one.

Chapter Two

Bringing Order to Funerals

The experience of loss is usually chaotic: the funeral is the first public expression of grief. It is a time of mourning that restores order and meaning to the funeral journey for believers.

When the *Order of Christian Funerals* was promulgated in 1989, there was considerable happiness that we had moved beyond a very lengthy interim rite. It had been a long twenty years to wait for this new ritual.[5] Everyone scrutinized what was in the ritual, and the result was some very mixed reviews.

There was a variety of perspectives about this new *Order of Christian Funerals*. Some were wondering what really made this any different from the interim rite. Others voiced concerns about the prayers and the appropriateness of replacing the interim ones. Still others wondered how the "stations," or "ritual moments," in the funeral journey could ever be implemented.

The preceding are some of the major questions levied not only in 1989 but that also, in many ways, still linger in our present time. We need to reflect and analyze what has been happening with this ritual.

---

5 Terence Curley, "Bringing Order to Funerals," *The Priest*, Vol.52, No. 11, Nov. 1996, p. 12

The intent of the *Order of Christian Funerals* is provided in the introduction. Appreciation of the rite requires familiarity with this important overview, but criticism is sometimes given by people who have not really done their homework and read the introduction. The introduction spells out in detail the place of the ritual in the believing community.

There have been far-reaching consequences for parish life stemming from the new ritual. In the past and in the interim rite, emphasis was on the mechanics of the rite and the priest's prayer options. Now it is collaboration within the parish. The rite urges priests, deacons, pastoral associates, musicians, funeral directors, and all parishioners to truly care for the bereaved. The community is called not only to bury its dead but also to minister to those left burdened by the loss.

Certainly, from the very earliest days of the Church, there has existed a ministry to the bereaved. There are important passages concerning widows and orphans in the Scriptures. Acts of love and other empathic responses have always been essential components for a believing community. The Ministry of Consolation as it is named in the ritual is to care for those suffering from separation and loss. Some of the outstanding aspects of the ritual follows.

A Better Connection

The rite emphasizes the importance of connecting our rituals to pastoral care. This could be termed "liturgical/pastoral theology." There is a practical tone to the ritual that has made all the difference for grief ministry. Grief ministers are provided with tools to work with the bereaved in ways that assist them to place loss into the context of faith.

Taking the Journey

The ritual creates some meaningful images for anyone experiencing loss. It is in keeping with the spirit and words of Vatican II. The role of the People of God as expressed in *Lumen Gentium* ("Light of the People") is very clearly given. In this document, the Council speaks to members as a pilgrim people. We realize as we celebrate this ritual that not only are we pilgrims traveling together but also companions on the journey who are to aid one another on this journey of life and faith.

New Directions

No journey may be completed when everyone wants to go in a different direction. Most important of all is the fact that we cannot bypass companions. We must bring them with us All of the totems and taboos of our death denying culture contribute to the exclusion of the bereaved, but the ritual acts as a compass that gives everyone direction. It is rooted in scripture and prayerfully introduces those who mourn with the reality of ongoing pastoral care from the community of faith.

Ministry and Participation

The ministry of consolation ensures for the Church that grief will always be experienced in a sacred manner. This is a vital concern in a society that secularizes everything. The message is that faith and the resources of faith are not something merely "added on" to the grieving process. Rather, the resolution of grief, with a healing and healthy outcome, depends on the faith perspective. After all, we as Christians believe "we walk by faith, not by sight."

New Resources in Faith

The Order of Christian Funerals depends upon the ministry of the community to fulfill its ways of healing. We have in the preceding chapter emphasized the call to minister caring for the bereaved at the death of a Christian is a ministry for all to participate in as members of the Body of Christ.

The ritual likens the funeral itself to being a short journey. There are stops along the way, and these stops are called "stations." For this to happen effectively, parish leadership has to nurture ministries. Liturgical planning, special prayers before the vigil, and many other options given at the time of the funeral are always in need of the community's participation.

Some of the difficulties associated with implementing the ritual originate with the misunderstanding that the ordained ministry has to do everything. When this attitude prevails, the community cannot really celebrate the intent of the ritual to fill the time during the short journey with prayers for the deceased and the bereaved.

My earliest recollection of the promulgation of the ritual is of the resources that came forward from the community. I was in a parish where a psychologist, a registered nurse, and a pastoral associate all minister together, sharing a new vision from the ritual. While I am certain that this was unusual, it nevertheless highlights the gifts that the parish community has and is willing to share.

The results of the collaboration were a parish caring (or support) group, pastoral visitations, liturgical planning, hospitality for the bereaved, and special liturgies. This is occurring in more and more parishes throughout the country. Through the ministry, the Gospel is being preached toward people's needs while they experience loss.

Resource and Reference for Grief Ministry

Since the promulgation of the *Order of Christian Funerals* (1989), there have been many secular books and a plethora of spiritual books dealing with bereavement. Collectively these titles address the multifaceted aspects of loss, ranging from the death of loved ones to deaths due to violence, disaster, accidents, sickness, or suicide, as well as other topics.

The ritual in many ways has acted as a catalyst for grief ministry. It includes a variety of way to ritualize losses. It is interesting to note that the ritual has a special section devoted to circumstances surrounding death. It has a personal dimension that speaks to grief. There are special prayers for parents of young people who have died; along with these prayers, there is a special liturgy for the death of a child. We will explore in future chapters the pastoral/liturgical dimensions associated with such losses.

Dialoging with God

Our spiritual life is given a rich resource in the ritual. Particular attention is given to the psalms. The Office for the Dead

(Part IV, *Order of Christian Funerals*) is a very significant aspect of the ritual. It fosters a realization that the Prayer of the Church relates in a healing way to the needs of the bereaved. Celebrating the hours as a community acknowledges "the spiritual bond that links the Church on earth with the Church in heaven, for it is in union with the whole Church that this prayer is offered on behalf of the deceased" (*Order of Christian Funerals,* par. 349).

The faith of the psalms helps us during critical times. Grief ministry depends on the psalms to help those who need to express their innermost personal emotions. The psalms offer a way to acknowledge and own our emotions, expressing them in the context of faith. This is a wonderful contribution for grief ministry in the ritual.

Spiritual Growth

Bereavement is a time for transformation. The ritual is the beginning of a new way of relating to the loved one who has died, to others, to our own outlook, and to our relationships, especially our relationship with God. Moving from the physical presence to remembrance and the entire world of loved one is a spiritual concern. It is a spiritual evolution for us. We move to establish a new bond and new relationship with those who have gone before us in faith.

Ritualizing Our Losses

The world has been marked by many losses. Airplane and automobile accidents, along with disasters both natural and perpetrated by terrorism all in their aftermath display a necessity to ritualize the loss. Real healing occurs when we appreciate ritual as a healing vehicle. Ritual words and actions facilitate the grieving process. In many ways the *Order of Christian Funerals* acts as a compass as we negotiate our ways through the chaotic time of loss. It brings direction and order to the grief experience.

Crisis Ministry

Ministry is a necessity during critical times if we are to be present to those who are suffering During those times the Gospel has to be proclaimed to the point of people's needs.

The ministry of consolation has been given insights from grief studies in our time. Ministry is assisted in having better ways to be present to those suffering the shock, especially that of sudden loss. Psychological information helps the ministry guide the bereaved in managing losses. It fulfills the vision of the ritual to realize that "when one member suffers, we all suffer."

Changing Burial Customs

The ritual addresses the changes that are occurring in our time with burial. Cremation has recently been added as an appendix in the ritual (see the chapter on "Cremation and Bodily Resurrection"). Other options include burial at sea. Our society needs to be educated in changes and these new options. Unfortunately, there are mistaken views, especially about the disposition of the cremated remains. The ritual ensures that dignity be given to the body for disposition, as the body is sacred in its creation and hope for resurrection.

Pastoral Action

This chapter has addressed salient features of the Order of Christian Funerals. These topics are to be kept in mind as we catechize and celebrate the funeral ritual. It is meant to help us at a critical time to realize that the ritual does assist us while we seek to experience healing for major hurts in our lives. We cannot be afraid to reach out to others who can implement this ministry. Parishioners have many skills that can be applied to this ministry. My earliest establishing of a support group relied on a psychologist, nurse, and pastoral associate to make the hope for this ministry become a reality for the parish. Not only do we invite parishioners who are in need, but also those parishioners who will shape the ministry of consolation. We have to avoid at all costs being a loner doing this ministry. A team effort is very effective and supportive.

Chapter Three

The Ritual's Symbols for Support

The importance of symbols and ways to appreciate what they mean is an essential aspect for appreciating the Catholic funeral. This chapter briefly explains the importance of symbols in the death of a Christian.

In the previous chapter, we see that there are a number of opportunities within the new rite to personalize the public expression of grief. When either the minister or the family seeks to do so, they should concentrate on the religious expressions the deceased utilized during his/her life. By doing so we broaden the context of grief. When using secular or non religious symbols, we ought to attempt to associate them with the religious whenever possible.

Religious symbols create a supportive, caring atmosphere during the time of the wake and the funeral ceremonies, though there are secular symbols that also contribute to the supportive tone of the funeral.[6]

Parishes are presently being challenged to implement ways to pray for the deceased and at the same time assist the living.

---

[6] Terence Curley, "Creating A Supportive Atmosphere for Funerals," *Pastoral Life,* vol.41, no.10, Nov. 1992

This is no small pastoral task. However, when we include the bereaved and allow them to participate, healing results occur.

The pastoral caregiver is both innovator and mediator when important personal symbols or details are requested. Both of these roles contribute to an overall countercultural identity, which is needed in our day.

The ritual is a necessary resource for pastoral caregivers. In order to develop a more personal ceremony it is good to rely on this ritual, which presents and explains many new options.

The general introduction to the *Order Of Christian Funerals* addresses the family and friends. The intent is to meet the needs of the bereaved in a more personal way, as the following highlights.

> In planning and carrying out the funeral rites the pastor and all other ministers should keep in mind the life of the deceased and the circumstances of death. They should also take into consideration the spiritual and psychological needs of the family and friends of the deceased to express grief and their sense of loss, to accept the reality of death and to comfort one another.
>
> (*Order Of Christian Funerals,* paragraph 16).

Those spiritual and psychological needs noted in the introduction are expressed through symbols. When meeting with the family that wants to personalize the funeral, the caregiver should bear the preceding quote in mind. Many symbols are allowed by the new ritual to assist the family in their grief work. The symbols may range from photographs to the family Bible.

Appropriate care and planning should be done about the placing of symbols in the funeral home, the parish church, and the place of committal. This means developing clear ideas of what the funeral home and the church will allow. Such planning should take place long before the pastoral caregiver has to communicate those options to the bereaved family. Some parishes are even developing printed guidelines similar to those used for marriage. Having such guidelines often avoids unnecessary confrontations or misunderstandings.

When we examine religious symbols in the public expression of loss, the distinction between grieving and mourning can be helpful. Becoming aware of the psychodynamics better equips us to relate to those who are suffering an intense loss.

Grief refers to those very personal subjective feelings and behaviors that attend the conscious recognition of loss. Grieving refers essentially to a personal experience and to the particular constellation of feelings and behavioral responses that characterize an indiviual.[7]

Mourning is given another definition:

Mourning, on the other hand refers to the "social face of grief" (Parkes,) personal communicationOctober,1983). It involves social and cultural expressions of grief and specific mourning practices. These are viewed as ways of demonstrating love forand devotion to the deceased and in many respects are felt by the bereaved person to be a duty.[8]

---

[7] Walter Smith, S.J., *Dying in the Human Life Cycle, Psychological, Biomedical, and Social Perspectives,* N.Y..;:CBS College Publishing, 1985, p.166.
[8] Ibid..167.

Every society contributes to the ritualizing of loss. We ought to approach the new ritual realizing that ethnic expressions and beliefs are integral aspects of the way people grieve. We can learn a great deal from cross-cultural investigations about grief. By doing so, we will not only learn differences but become more culturally sensitive to alternate expressions. How people dress and relate to others during times of grief and mourning assists them in being aware and adjusting to loss. In this way, we can learn how to help the bereaved to become aware of their losses.

I recall going to a household in a poor housing project in Boston. The South American family was experiencing the sudden death of the father. Being new in the parish, I had presumed that I'd find out what funeral parlor to go to and what prayers to be offered. You can imagine my surprise when I walked into a small apartment and saw many adults and children crowded into the living room. Some cooked, others ate a special traditional meal, and little children ran around while the body was laid out on a table in the kitchen.

This family's culture called for an intimate association with the deceased during the grief process. While at first it seemed strange to me, I even thought it may have been callous, after a short time my eyes were opened. Looking closer, I could see genuine grief taking place. While life continued, the deceased was intimately attended to by family members; through gestures and touches, the deceased father remained close. The family was acknowledging that this was a time of passage. Caring and participation was strong among the mourners.

Accepting loss entails considerable community support. We have to be concerned that the limited social and cultural supports for the bereaved in Western societies make it very difficult for the bereaved to process their emotions. We have to develop a perspective towards the funeral ritual that emphasizes healing through expression.

Certain tasks to facilitate grief are necessary for the bereaved. Since this is the initial phase of the grief work, it is important to begin with a healthy perspective to assist the bereaved in adapting to this crisis.

Symbols especially help in the initial phase of grief work. They assist the bereaved in remembering the deceased loved one. At the same time, they allow the necessary letting go. There is a mixture between the secular and sacred symbol while grieving. These symbols become, in effect, transitional objects that the bereaved use while their relationship with the deceased is transforming itself. Because of this mixture, there can be a tension between the two, which will be minimized by having clear options available for the placement of symbols. Personal photographs in the funeral home may contribute to a more caring atmosphere. A family album, a newspaper clipping, an obituary, even a favorite fishing rod is respecting the memory of the loved one in an appropriate way. Family members are able to recall happier times and accomplishments. The conversations these engender at the gathering of friends and relatives are more in tune with the deceased person's life.

The correct setting establishes what is appropriate and respectful for a personal funeral. The religious symbols may be prominent at the funeral home, church, and cemetery; the secular symbols may be appropriate at other times.

Religious Symbols

In the new ritual, religious symbols are abundant. There are guidelines for their use that require care to be taken when using them. Within the ritual there are times set aside for the use of symbols. Let us briefly outline those times that allow for the use of symbols within the funeral rite.

The beginning of the funeral offers the option of placing the pall on the casket. This ritual option has given new meaning to the "pall bearers." They can perform the action or family members can. In recent times this option has proven to be meaningful to many families. There is a sense of caring for the loved one that hearkens back to the days of family members dressing the body for burial.

The symbolism here reflects the clothing of the person at baptism when a white garment was used to designate the new life of the Christian. This symbol reappears at the Christian's death when he is bringing that white garment, as the Rite of Baptism states, "unstained into the everlasting life of heaven."

In the past, this action was always performed by the priest. Now an option in the new ritual allows for the bereaved to place the pall.

> If it is the custom in the local community, a pall may be placed over the coffin when it is received at the church. A reminder of the baptismal garment of the deceased, the pall is a sign of the Christian dignity of the person. The use of the pall also signifies that all are equal in the eyes of God. [see James 2:1-9
>
> (*Order Of Christian Funerals,* par.,38)

The placing of the family Bible on the casket draped with the white pall is another important way of participating. This highlights the importance of the word of God for the Christian, as well as the family memories attached to it. Faithfulness to the word and its message leads to eternal life.

The family may decide to place a family crucifix or rosary beads on top of the pall. The cross symbolizes that all Christians are signed with the sign of the cross at baptism. Jesus suffered on the cross and was uplifted by the resurrection. So, too, the Christians participating in the funeral can identify with suffering. They need the consolation and hope of the resurrection to be clearly evident. The rosary beads, while a personal object of private prayer, certainly convey the message of devotion to Mary.

During the funeral, it is essential that the community realize there are many bonds of friendship. The funeral is a time of realizing that a very real affective bond has been broken. There remain, however, many ties that continue. These relationships are especially important during this time of loss, as is clearly evident when a friend or family member accepts the role of lector or reader during the funeral mass. Those reticent to take on this role may be assisted by the priest or funeral director who agrees to signal when it is time to go to the podium.

The family may wish to do the readings and intercessions themselves or designate someone to represent the family. It is a personal honor for someone to be asked to proclaim the scripture reading at this time. The family may also request special prayers in the prayers of the faithful. While the deceased is remembered and prayed for, the family may request that other deceased family members be prayed for within these prayers.

An example of this would be a family requesting that a prayer be said for a deceased father at their mother's funeral. The pastoral caregiver assists the family by reminding them of this opportunity early. By doing so, he helps that family become adequately prepared.

Remembering others who have died comforts the bereaved. As we have spiritually redefined our relationship with those who previously died, so, too, must we do so now. Redefining our relationships with those who die is one of the most significant tasks for grief work. This redefining ought to start as soon as possible. By including other deceased family members in the prayers of petition we place this new loss in the broader context of family losses that we have experienced and resolved.

Families may participate in the procession of the gifts. The gifts of the altar breads, water, and wine to be used in the liturgy are usually placed on a table away from the altar and brought up by members of the congregation after the readings. This procession reminds the community that these gifts symbolize our bringing ourselves and our deeds to the altar of the Lord. This can be a meaningful time for families. Very often the family will continue the service begun with the placing of the pall and help set the table for the Eucharist. Frequently the family will designate some members as the bearers of gifts. A growing tradition seems to be the choice of the youngest family members. This may be especially meaningful for the family at the funeral of a grandparent. In addition to the gifts of bread and wine, the family also has the option of being creative and working on grief issues in personalizing the gifts for placement on the altar.

We ought to invite the grandchildren to show their love. It would hardly be out of place for a grandchild to bring up a drawing or a favorite gift. The drawing chosen may have been in the grandparent's kitchen. There is a need for the child to adjust to the loss, and this symbolic action is helpful. The cross or rosary placed on the pall could now be placed on the altar.

Liturgy is meant to help the bereaved to release emotions. A rigid or controlling approach only stultifies emotions. Real healing occurs when people are able to let go of their pain by crying out. We cannot be afraid of this kind of ritualizing Everyone ought to be invited to participate to the best extent they can. This means even the youngest members of the family.

The final farewell at the conclusion of the liturgy is a special time for remembrances. It is here when someone may do a remembrance or farewell. This is not a eulogy. It is meant to be a recalling of the Christian's life and its meaning for the community. There are intensely personal aspects that may be recalled. They include the deceased's role as a parent, friend, confidant, and member of the parish community. If a family chooses to designate someone to do a remembrance, the pastoral caregiver can assist by sharing guidelines from the parish.

The pastoral caregiver can assist whoever is designated to read a remembrance. The farewell is meant as a way of remembering and at the same time letting go of an effective bond. Once again, we note how certain actions help us to redefine our relationship with those who have died.

The farewell is not meant to be a long treatise or a eulogy. Rather, it is a way of recalling how the loved one lived as a Christian. This may be accomplished by recalling or retelling family and personal stories that provide insights to the theme of the deceased Christian's life. The time of farewell develops ways for the bereaved to grieve by recollecting significant events and relationships attached to the deceased. At the same time, it also fulfills an important aspect of grief work.

When someone close to us dies, they are more present in our minds than perhaps at any other time. We recall events and characteristics we would other wise not think about. This kind of recalling is one of the major symptoms associated with grief. The ritual allows us to act this out by setting aside time for saying goodbye.

The prayers at the time of farewell provide us with comforting images of our bonding with the deceased amid future hope. The very tone for the farewell is set by ritual in the following words:

> Before we go our separate ways, let us take leave of our brother/sister. May our farewell express our affection for him/her; may it ease our sadness and strengthen our hope. One day we shall joyfully greet him/her again when the love of Christ, which conquers all things, destroys even death itself.

(Order Of Christian Funerals, par. 171).

The Ritual and How to Include Secular Symbols

We noted that secular symbols also have a place in the funeral. They, too, contribute to the psychological well being of the bereaved. Remembering that a loved one was a member of certain associations national organizations or was a veteran are all part of the loved one's personal history that the family may want to focus on. While recognizing that these symbols have merit, the Church makes some important distinctions on their use. In treating the funeral as a process, the Church is not excluding their use; rather, it is designating times when other symbols become paramount. The ritual therefore states:

> Only Christian symbols may rest on or be placed near the coffin during the funeral liturgy. Any other symbols, for example, national flags, or flags or insignia of associations, have no place in the funeral liturgy [see no.132]

(Order Of Christian Funerals, par. 38).

The reference to paragraph 132 is the following:

> Any national flags or the flags or insignia of associations to which the deceased belonged are to be removed from the coffin at the entrance of the church. They may be replaced after the coffin has been taken from the church.

(Order Of Christian Funerals. Par 132).

In the Catholic funeral, these directives have caused not a little difficulty among funeral directors. Interpretation of the ritual is very significant for a personal way of remembering the individual. The second paragraph (132) illustrates that the secular symbol is not excluded. It is being placed into context. What has to be emphasized is that there are different symbols and times for their use. It is not to repudiate patriotism that the national flag is not in the liturgical ceremony in the church. The flag may be shown at the funeral home and the cemetery. By excluding the national or civil focus in the church, the ritual is returning to the theme that the deceased is now beyond these things. He/she now stands on the threshold of eternity. It is here that our destiny lies. In some ways this could be considered countercultural since the deceased is beyond it.

Symbols relating to the mysteries of faith take precedence in the Roman Catholic liturgy. This is in keeping with liturgical norms ensuring that the personal encounter with God and among members be spiritual. The pastoral caregiver is doing a service to the bereaved family and the Church when explanations are provided to the bereaved so that they understand the distinction being made.

This chapter has cited some of the significant times for personal responses within the Roman Catholic ritual. As was previously noted, the pastoral caregiver, whether a minister or community member, is a key person in the planning and enacting of events. This is an important responsibility. The new ritual, by allowing the community to take on the role of explaining and facilitating, has significantly enhanced the meaning of community. At the same time, when new options are chosen, a more personal, meaningful funeral results.

The following gives an overview of those circumstances where the family may use symbols to personalize the funeral.

How to Use Symbols for Healing and Hope

1. Family religious objects ought to be utilized during the ritual. Religious objects may include the loved one's or another's rosary beads, cross or crucifix, and family Bible. These are used at the funeral home within the funeral liturgy and at the cemetery. Later, when looking at the object, new meaning is given to it in light of this use. For those families

that cannot readily find a meaningful religious object, they may chose to acquire a new one that will be changed by its use within the funeral.
2. The use of secular symbols from organizations, clubs, fraternal orders, unions, etc. is an option, according to the funeral director's discretion at the Funeral home and cemetery. Special guidelines apply to their use in church. Flags may be used throughout the funeral with the exception of the church service.
3. Family members or friends may be designated to place the pall on the casket during the funeral liturgy. This ritual recalls baptism and provides the family with an expression of care.
4. Those helping the family arrange the funeral ought to realize the need to include close family friends in the liturgy. The lector for readings and prayers of the faithful may be chosen by the family. The family may personalize the prayers of the faithful by asking that additional family members be remembered in prayers.
5. Grandchildren or other close relatives and friends may be designated to bring up the gifts; water, wine, a chalice, or other personal items, e.g., a drawing from a young child, may be included.
6. The family may designate a family member or friend to offer two or three typed pages of recollection about the deceased as a Christian. This may be read at the final farewell. Some families have opted not to read a farewell. Instead they have printed memorial pamphlets outlining the funeral mass and included a written remembrance in it. In the future, this aspect of saying goodbye may well take place at the vigil or at the family reception at the end of the funeral journey.

There has been considerable feedback about how this farewell is often misunderstood, and inappropriate remarks within the church's sacred setting are not appreciated.
7. Special symbols or requests at the cemetery may be chosen by family. What ought to be remembered is that the ministry and participation during the funeral means explaining symbols and facilitating their use.

A meaningful celebration is always more than just assigning roles for people. It is truly directing, participating, and ministering to others during the liturgies of Christian burial. The funeral liturgy, the final commendation, and the committal are significant moments that require a meaningful expression of respect and love by the community of believers.

Pastoral Action

Ministry and participation are essential for good liturgical worship. As pastoral ministers we are called to do the best we can to include the bereaved in meaningful ways to worship. The symbols serve a very important role for those who are grieving. They are ritual objects that provide a deep sense of participation. For example, in placing the pall on the casket, they are truly caring for their loved one at the funeral. It is more than important for them to have a funeral that is personal and to care for the last time for the physical body of their loved one. Also, the ritual helps in accepting the loss and expressing their love for the deceased by doing an action that is significant for the end of their spiritual journey here on earth.

Chapter Four

Phases in Grief Ministry

Developing a pastoral plan for responding to the community's needs is essential for parishes. I f we are to be effective, there is a need to be familiar with ways to provide skilled interventions for others during critical times. This chapter outlines phases for effectively including the bereaved in parish life.

"Crisis ministry" is the term for a specific kind of pastoral care. It means ministering to people when they are experiencing a crisis. This ministry was enlightened by crisis-intervention techniques developed for psychology.

The Cocoanut Grove nightclub fire in Boston on Saturday evening, November 28,1942 initiated studies about grief. What was to be an evening of merrymaking following college football games turned into tragedy. It was a sudden fire originating in the cocktail lounge. The burning was complicated by poisonous smoke from the draperies and furnishings. Panic struck the crowd as the exits were blocked by jammed revolving doors. It only took a few minutes for the death toll to reach four hundred and eighty-one. Another one hundred and eighty-one people were seriously injured. This fire in Boston initiated new laws for safe exits, a legal limit to the number of people in a public dwelling, and the compliance of laws curtailing flammable materials in public halls.

The magnitude of the fire was the precipitating event for caring and chronicling grief among the survivors and relatives of the victims. Since then, many of the symptoms and the way people grieve have been investigated.

Two researchers Dr. Eric Lindeman and Dr. Gerald Caplan pioneered new ways of relating to the bereaved. By observing the reactions of the bereaved, they gained insights into common reactions to a crisis situation with the hope of finding ways to help people cope. They were able to suggest that there are timeframes for initial intense reactions to grief. Certain symptoms, both physical and emotional, are common (according to their observations) for approximately six to eight weeks. Active liturgical and crisis ministry mirrors this timeframe. There are ways to help people accept their losses and manage grief. The new ritual provides a foundation for a comprehensive way to guide the bereaved, and the ritual's vision connects rituals with pastoral care.

When we consider what is normative for intense grief and associate it with ritual and pastoral actions, we realize how significant the *Order Of Christian Funerals* is for parishes. By adapting the phases of grief to pastoral care, we can readily appreciate how caregivers can aid the bereaved to pass through grief. These are broken down to the following phases: (1) initial phase (intervention with the grief-stricken), (2) second phase (liturgical preparation), (3) third phase (pastoral visits), and (4) fourth phase (parish support group/grief seminar).

(1) Initial Phase (Intervening with the Grief Stricken)

This phase is characterized by reactions on the part of the bereaved and the caregiver. News of the death of a loved one initiates reactions of shock, denial, numbness, and disorientation amid the need to make arrangements for the funeral. This is the time when the pastoral caregiver meets with the bereaved. The pastoral meeting may occur at the deceased's home, hospital, or the funeral home.

When the pastoral caregiver meets with the family, it is the beginning of the final journey for the deceased. The caregiver represents the community of believers who will journey with the family and friends according to the significant moments or stations in the ritual.

The pastoral caregiver is present at this time when the bereaved are coping with arrangements and other practical details. The pastor or pastoral caregiver plays an important role in the bereaved accepting the reality of loss. They are there to assist them in sharing feelings. This symbolic presence of a representative of the parish community interacting with the family illustrates for them the reality of the loss.

(2) Second Phase (Preparing the Funeral Liturgy)

Within the initial period of shock, there is the need for the bereaved to interact with society. Our culture starts the clock of grief work running. For our death denying society, the viewpoint of that timeframe only covers the intense period of grief. This time demands that the body be removed, prepared, and buried in short order. We as a true community, walk the thin line of helping the bereaved by lending focus to these cultural demands. It is also during this time the pastoral caregiver helps the bereaved to prepare the liturgy.

An empathic response from the caregiver communicates care and considerable consolation. The family needs options for participating in the liturgies surrounding the burial of their loved one. Appropriate scriptural readings may be selected. In making selections from scripture, the pastoral caregiver may utilize this activity to read and pray with the bereaved.

This is a critical time and the pastoral caregiver has to assess the intensity of the grief and provide comfort. The images and reality of care are best communicated by the scriptures. The role of the Psalms and certain responses, such as feelings of abandonment, anger, sadness, and yearning, may be noted. This helps the bereaved to identify and begin to process their feelings. (See the chapter on Biblical roots.)[9]

The burial liturgies are events that assist the grieving process. The symbols experienced in faith give a dimension to the meaning of loss in the Christian perspective. Liturgy relates in an ongoing way to assist the bereaved in remembering and respecting the loved one who has died. It redefines the bereaved relationship with the deceased in the comforting context of the Reign of God and the Communion of Saints.

(3) Third Phase (Pastoral Visits to the Bereaved)

Once the funeral is concluded, our culture demands that life return to normal. It is here that we encounter the 'leper

---

[9] Terence Curley, "Psalms for Separation and Loss," *The Priest*, vol. 47, no.11, Nov. 1991, p. 41

like' reaction people have toward the bereaved. Because society demands that life be back to normal, many people shun the bereaved or the topic of loss. It is the role of the caregiver to contend that there is no artificial time limit for grief. It is normal to express grief no matter what the culture says. The very presence of the caregiver is an acknowledgement that grief continues and must be addressed.

A pastoral visit may be scheduled approximately two weeks after the funeral. This illustrates another dimension of pastoral care In this way, pastoral care is experienced as the response of pastor and congregation to parishioners at a critical time. The parish is seen as serving the needs of the bereaved, not just providing a service or liturgy and subsequently forgetting about them.

When intervening or responding to the bereaved, some aspects ought to be borne in mind. If we are to be effective in our visit, we should be mindful of how we respond. There are immanent and transcendent aspects of a pastoral visit.

Immanence describes our being with troubled people in an empathic way, not in the way as an obstacle.[10] The caregiver should not feel constrained to control the situation. He/she should be there mainly to listen and, when appropriate, guide the bereaved to examine different viewpoints. On the other hand, transcendent means our being sufficiently detached from the situation. This allows us to make assessments, identify goals, and discover ways to facilitate growth. The combination of both aspects is helpful for the pastoral caregiver doing crisis ministry.

---

10 Homer Jernigan, "Immanence and Transcendence in Pastoral Care, Some Basic Considerations," *Journal of Pastoral Care*, June 1984, pp. 120-132

The transcendent aspect allows the pastoral person to be aware of both the normal and abnormal embracing of grief. It is necessary to remember normal tasks that range from coping with the initial loss to reinvesting in human relationships and participating in the community or social affairs. It is likewise important to be aware of abnormal responses to grief. This is the detachment that allows the pastor to assess, monitor, intervene, and follow up on care for the bereaved.

The pastoral caregiver ought to acknowledge that there are situations when there is an abnormal response to grief. Some of the characteristics are: being overwhelmed by pain, avoiding or denying the pain, or clinging to the pain. When the pastor feels that the person is not coping then a professional referral may have to be done.

The following pastoral example illustrates what we can expect when we visit certain grief stricken people in need of referral.

Edith's son Karl died suddenly six months ago. Since then, all she does is think about him. All of her conversations consist of mentioning him. Somehow everything is associated with his memory. Lately she has had considerable memory loss. Edith has had trouble sleeping and does not eat very well. The pastoral visitor noticed that the strain was s really showing on her face. Edith appeared to be withdrawing rather than reorganizing her life.

The pastoral visit is an example of doing crisis ministry. There is a theological aspect to intervention that is biblical. The Bible is the Book of the Acts of God. It is God's intervention into our lives in the history of salvation. Similarly; we are called to intervene into the lives of others.

Grief ministry in the parish is assisted by crisis intervention techniques. The intersecting of psychology and theology occurs when ministry is practiced in this way. This pastoral practice of having a caregiver and the community utilizes resources to bring healing for those who otherwise would be on their own in our culture.

Crisis ministry benefits parishioners during pastoral visits. It is a way of being present (immanent) and helping them to cope. At the same time, to be really helpful, assessing the needs and degree of coping (transcendent aspect) is necessary.

Dr. Howard Parad, another pioneer of crisis intervention, describes what the intervention accomplishes

> Crisis-intervention means entering into the life situation of an individual, family, or group to alleviate the impact of a crisis-inducing stress in order to help mobilize the resources of those directly affected, as well as those who are in the "significant social orbit," to use Lindeman's term. The intervener has the dual objective of (1) reducing, whenever possible, the impact of the stressful event, and (2) utilizing the crisis situation to help those affected not only to solve present problems but also to become strengthened in mastering future vicissitudes by the use of more effective adaptive coping mechanisms.[11]

If the pastoral caregiver is with the bereaved during the funeral, all efforts are usually more effective. During the pastoral visit, references may be made to the funeral and ritual actions. This reminds the bereaved of reality and helps to avoid denial.

---

[11] Howard J. Parad, *Crisis Intervention: Selected Readings*, New York: Family Service Assoc. of America, 1966, p. 2

Also, the process of moving from chaos to resuming normal activities is facilitated by going over events. The bereaved begin to see that they are not still at "square one."

Lee Ann Hoff lists some intervention strategies:
1. *Listen actively and with concern.*
2. *Encourage the open expression of feelings.*
3. *Help the person gain an understanding of the crisis.*
4. *Help the individual gradually accept reality.*
5. *Help the person explore new ways of coping.*[12]

During the weeks and months following the funeral, support has to be provided for families. There is an ongoing need for pastoral care as the bereaved try to sort out their emotions and develop coping techniques.

Developing a pastoral perspective for bereavement care requires examining our assumptions about ministry. Six assumptions that apply to grief ministry are given by Dr. Homer Jernigan. These assumptions are operative throughout the funeral journey and the subsequent time of bereavement. I have noted how in some respects the assumptions directly relate to grief.[13]

1. There is in every person the innate (God given) drive to grow. The caregiver helps the person not to be "stuck" or "blocked' in growth. The caregiver does this by asking the right questions while being with the person. The questions may be about how they are doing in coping with the death.

---

[12] Lee Ann Hoff, *People in Crisis, Understanding and Helping*, Addison-Wesley Publishing Co., Reading, MA, 1984, p.118.
[13] Homer Jernigan, "Ministry With The Aging: A Cross Cultural Perspective," Boston, MA, Boston University Papers, 1989, p.75

These questions may be weaved into the meeting in creative and sensitive ways. Lee Ann Hoff's intervention strategies for the crisis are helpful in this regard.

2. A primary purpose in ministry is to enable the personal growth (of all ages) in love of God, neighbor, and self. There is a need to be able to love again in the process of doing grief work. As this occurs the deceased becomes reintegrated into the life of the bereaved in a new, loving perspective.

3. There are important needs for continual personal growth. In bereavement ministry, this applies to ongoing care or, in psychological terms, "post-vention." This is part of the reaffirmation of life.

4. Different cultures possess varying understandings of personal growth. The cross-cultural approach is appropriate for appreciating wholeness in doing ministry. This relates to race, ethnicity, age, gender, economic status, and other variations that affect grief work. These are important considerations for the caregiver to make an effort to understand in the context of grief.

5. Ministry has to continually evaluate personal growth. This relates to the transcendent or detached way of assessing and assists in recognizing the needs of the bereaved. Step back but don't t step out of the picture. What works well for many is to spend some time alone after the visit to re-examine what occurred; others write notes and then review them later to keep perspective.

6. In ministry, forms of community life have to be developed to counteract cultural weakness. The pastoral visit cultivates a feeling of belonging to the parish. We as Christians need to band together in love and support as the Church. This assumption is important for building community.

(4) Fourth Phase (Parish Caring Group)

The parish caring/support group is an expression of ongoing pastoral care. It is a covenant or an agreement with the bereaved to be present to them in their bereavement. This entails sharing feelings and viewpoints for growing through troubled times.

A caring group may become a microcommunity of the parish. This is a goal in fostering interdependence among members. Participating in this form of community life helps the bereaved to go through the grieving process.

Caring groups are not only for sharing feelings. By their nature they are for growth and perspective. Group activities and topics help those seeking to reaffirm faith during the terrible experience of loss. Bereavement groups or seminars review some matters related managing loss. One topic for discussion may be a review of the funeral. How the group experienced the liturgies or significant moments helps with acceptance. Both positive and negative feelings ought to be explored. Feelings of anger, abandonment, and confusion may well be directed toward God. This is a significant topic for discussion. The bereaved need a forum to freely express what otherwise they would either deny, be afraid to mention, or fail to accept.

Dr. Howard Clinebell has done considerable work with groups. He outlines some specific tasks associated with the process of going through grief

1. *Accept the reality of the loss.*
2. *Experience and talk about painful feelings.*

3. Put life back together (through making choices and constructive actions.)
4. Put the loss into the wider context of faith.
5. Reach out for mutual help to others who are grieving.[14]

The parish support group is one healing vehicle among the ways we can reach out and include the bereaved. What is expressed by having such a group is the continuation of a pastoral vision stemming from the new ritual. The responsibility for pastoral care rests with the believing community. This is asserted by the *Order Of Christian Funerals* (par. 9) when it states that we are called as members of the Body of Christ to be supportive and consoling. This is in keeping with: "Blessed are they who mourn; they shall be consoled." (Matt. 5:3).

If we are to have truly effective pastoral care for the bereaved, it means charting the way through grief's chaotic storms.[15] This pastoral overview for practicing grief ministry serves as a bridge over troubled waters needed to include the grief stricken in the community's life. Meeting the bereaved amidst the chaos contributes to the transformation of grief into the grace of acceptance and investing in life once again. No longer is there an embracing of darkness. Rather, there is light provided by the empowering presence of the Holy Spirit active among believers.

---

14 Howard Clinebell and Martha Hickman, "Growing Through Grief: Personal Healing," U.M. Com. Productions, Nashville, Part 2, *The Five Tasks of Grief Work*, Video/VHS
15 Terence Curley, *Planning The Catholic Funeral*, Collegeville Ministry Series, Collegeville, MA, 2005

Pastoral Action

Every parish needs to have pastoral plans for ministry. This chapter outlines salient points for ways to minister to the bereaved not only at the time of the funeral but also during the days, weeks, months and further. The early phases of grief require our support and awareness of their needs. Being present to the bereaved entails being aware of what is usually needed in our parishes. The ministry has to be ongoing, providing ways for the bereaved to "sort things out." Sorting things out is really a task of trying to experience peace even when we cannot fully understand everything. When we make a pastoral visit, we help people by being present to them to have someone who is willing to listen to their story. This chapter is geared toward helping the pastoral person to be an effective pastoral visitor by seeing the overall plan for ministry to the bereaved.

Chapter Five

Selecting Scripture for Liturgies

This chapter highlights the importance of selecting scripture for the liturgies surrounding the death of a Christian. The healing realities of revelation directly relate to ways for healing for the broken-hearted.

Choosing appropriate scripture readings can considerably enhance funeral liturgies. When families gather together and select readings for their loved one's funeral, such preparation facilitates essential grief work. It also is a significant endeavor for planning the Catholic funeral in a meaningful way.[16]

The scriptures focus the bereaved on healing images. This often happens when we identify with the familiar words that ground our beliefs in life. Our needs to remember, to reflect on suffering, separation, and loss, and to cry out are possible when we gather as families and explore the scriptures.

In choosing readings that relate to loss, there is no disguising of feelings. The word touches us. The dynamism reveals our innermost emptiness. The word of God in its revelation gives

---

16 Terence Curley, *Planning The Catholic Funeral*, The Liturgical Press, Collegeville, MN, 2005 Special attention to Appendix 3, Scripture Selection Guide, pp. 28-33

us permission to express our hurt, to cry out, even while we express our faith in God.

One evening not so long ago, I visited a family to prepare the liturgy for a deceased loved one. William was the father of the family and was loved as the patriarch. He was a friend and mentor to all of his six children and their spouses. Even though William had heart trouble, his death occurred after a long and painful struggle with cancer. The family loved him with untold intensity until the time of death. As a family, they had taken turns with vigils at the hospital. I knew that there would be a mixture of feelings in the way they would respond to the death. There was no doubt in my mind that relief and still intense pain at the death would be evident.

It was early evening when I arrived. The little children were still awake and not fully aware of what it meant that their grandfather had died. I spoke with some of the older teenage grandchildren, who were crying. They were invited to participate with their parents in the liturgy preparation. The little children went downstairs to play in the Family room while we went into the living room.

It was a time of sadness, especially as the children gathered leaving what was the father's special chair empty. When the widow came into the room, she very graciously took that chair. That gesture alone set the tone for the gathering. I could not help but experience a changing family ritual. As the family settled in, I re-explained that there are a variety of options in the new ritual.

These major liturgical events require the presence of the scriptures. The readings for the funeral mass are taken from the Old Testament, a Psalm, a New Testament Epistle, and the Gospel. A list of possible readings is available in the *Order Of Christian Funerals* (part III, par. 343). The ritual notes that the texts for scripture are interchangeable.

The ministry of participation is clearly evident with the recommendation that the minister consult with the family and close friends for choosing texts. It further notes that the texts ought to "most closely reflect the particular circumstances and the needs of the mourners" (*O.C.F.* par. 344).

By referring to another section (par. 397), we can utilize prayers and text that most closely reflect the circumstances of the death and the person being grieved. These circumstances include children who died, parents, a married couple, a deceased non-Christian married to a Catholic, a sudden death, an accident, a violent death, an elderly person, death from suicide, and one who has died after a long illness. These prayers may be used in various rites throughout the funeral.

In working with the family who had lost their husband and father, we began with a prayer. The prayer from the ritual is moving and relates to the intense feeling of accepting all the losses that preceded the death. It is a proclaiming that the ordeal has ended for both the family and the deceased loved one.

> O God, you are water for our thirst and manna in our desert. We praise you for the life of William and bless your mercy that has brought his suffering to an end. Now we beg that same mercy to raise him to new life. Nourished by the food and drink of heaven, may he rest for ever in the joy of Christ our Lord.
>
> R. Amen. (*Order Of Christian Funerals,* par. 398 #40)

Ellen, the oldest daughter, who was a nurse, began to quietly cry. She regained her composure and said that the prayer really helped her to realize it was over. Immediately it was clear that the family needed to accept that the suffering had ended for their loved one. Now, the final journey with the rites of burial was beginning.

Another daughter, Doris, had taken a couple of scripture courses while in college. She suggested that a reading from the Book of Isaiah would be very meaningful.

> The spirit of the Lord is upon me, because the Lord has anointed me; He has sent me to bring glad tidings to the lowly to heal the brokenhearted, to proclaim liberty to captives and release to the prisoners, To announce a year of favor from the Lord and a day of vindication by our God to comfort all who mourn; To place on those who mourn in Zion a diadem instead of ashes, To give them oil of gladness in place of mourning a glorious mantle instead of a listless spirit. They will be called oaks of justice planted by the Lord to show his glory.[17]

(Isaiah 61:1-3)

The scripture reading provided the context for explaining an important aspect about grief. I knew that for the adults, with the exception of the widow, there had not been many deaths in the family. I reassured them that God does allow us to be transformed in our grief. The words of the prophet illustrate that while we will always remember our loved ones, we will also proceed through this time of sorrow. There is hope in realizing that the time for the intense feelings of grief cannot go on forever. This is often a hard concept for the bereaved. In some ways

---

[17] *The New American Bible*, World Bible Publishers, Iowa Falls, Iowa, 1976 (Is.61.1-30)

the community (caregiver) must give permission to adjust to this new experience. For some people, to let go of these intense feelings can engender feelings of guilt for not grieving enough. The hope is that by looking at the experience through scriptural faith, a broader perspective will be fostered to facilitate the readjustment in the face of loss. While grief remains, hope is growing. We will see our loved ones again. We can experience their presence in the Eucharistic community.

Everyone agreed that the selection from Isaiah was meaningful for them in light of the suffering. It helped them lend focus to their feelings of relief after the siege of a lengthy illness. It was indeed the good news that they needed to hear as they realized what they had gone through together.

After the Old Testament reading is a Psalm response. Before examining the Psalm, I gave some background information highlighting the importance of the Psalm in grief work.[18]

The Psalms are unique in their perspective. They draw us in through tone, cadence, and emotions. We are one with the Psalmist as we cry out in pain while we praise God. We are truly ourselves in our conversations, however halting, with God. We acknowledge that God knows us for all times. When we were knit in our mother's womb, He knew us. He knows our innermost self and loves us even when we suffer and ask why.

The Psalms are the hymn book of the people. When we proclaim the Psalms, we are really dialoguing with God from the depths of our being. Very often the Psalms allow us to express feelings of abandonment, searching, yearning to be with our loved ones, and even anger. All of these feelings are appropriate.

---

18 Terence Curley, "Psalms Voices of Loss During Times of Loss," *Pastoral Life*, Vol.48, No.5, May 1991, p. 31

In the Psalms we find the rocky path through the valley of darkness. It was suggested that in the days and weeks ahead, returning to the Psalms is very helpful as we grieve.

William's widow, Mary, made it known that she always loved to hear Psalm Twenty-Three. She recalled how, when other family members had died, that Psalm gave her strength. Everyone listened attentively as she spoke. It was clear that the children needed to receive guidance as to how to go through this unique experience for them as a family.

> The Lord is my shepherd; I shall not want. In verdant pastures he gives me repose; Beside restful waters he leads me; he refreshes my soul. He guides me in right paths for his name's sake. Even though I walk in the dark valley I fear no evil; for you are at my side With your rod and your staff that give me courage You spread the table before in the sight of my foes; You anoint my head with oil; my cup overflows. Only goodness and kindness follow mall the days of my life And I shall dwell in the house of the Lord for years to come.
>
> Psalm 23

After we read the Psalm, one of the sons recalled that he had seen it printed on a holy card as a remembrance for people who have died. Everyone agreed that Psalm Twenty-Three would be their choice as the prayer for William's cards. They would include it along with thank you notes for people who visited and helped.

It was suggested that the family read over that Psalm as a way of receiving guidance. I made the observation that healing images help as we grieve, and urged them to spend a little time thinking about the image of walking through a gloomy valley alone then to feel the Lord's strong presence, which makes the darkness give way to light. This light reveals restful green fields with gently flowing water. Standing in the presence of the Lord in this beautiful setting, we are encouraged to look around and see that we are not alone. Many are with us on our journey. We are traveling together with the Lord. This kind of prayer requires finding a quiet place and looking within our troubled spirits for the peace the Lord offers us.[19]

The next reading chosen by this family was from the New Testament. The reading was taken from St. Paul's letter to the early Church at Ephesus. St. Paul wrote this personal prayer to the small Church at Ephesus to help them grow in faith. The loss of a member of the generation that passed on in faith is clearly put into perspective. He writes:

> "That is why I kneel before the Father from whom every family in heaven and on earth takes its name and I pray that he will bestow on you gifts in keeping with the riches of his glory. May he strengthen you inwardly through the working of his Spirit. May Christ dwell in your hearts through faith and may charity be the root and foundation of your life. Thus you will be able to grasp fully, with all the holy ones, the breadth and length and height and depth of Christ's love, and experience this love which surpasses all knowledge, so that you may attain to the fullness of God himself. To him who's power now at work in us can do immeasurably more than we ask or imagine, to him be

---

19 Terence Curley, "Psalms for Rebuilding Trust and Hope," *Pastoral Life*, Vol.51, No. 6, June 2002, p.21

glory in the church and in Christ Jesus through all generations, world without end." Amen

Ephesians:3.14-21.3.

Once again the bond that exists among a family needs to be committed to prayer during the funeral liturgies. When the family is placed into the context of one generation passing on the flame of faith to the next generation, spiritual significance is given during the initial time of loss.

Just as one generation resembles the previous, so, too, does our faith, which is also passed on. This reading reminds us of our generation of faith and in doing so reflects the baptismal imagery within the funeral rite. When we speak of the passing on of faith, we recall the parents and godparents at baptism both making the sign of the cross on the infant's head, clothing the child in the white garment, which becomes the funeral pall, and holding the candle lit for the Paschal candle, which is again lit for the funeral.

The Gospel readings reflect Jesus ministry of consolation. The establishing of the Kingdom is our comfort and consolation We realize in faith that we are bonded together in the Body of Christ awaiting the completion of the Kingdom at the Second Coming.

The *Sermon On The Mount* was the reading selected from the Gospel options. We read this and reflected on what the words would mean when we heard them during the funeral mass.

"When he saw the crowds he went up on the mountainside. After he sat down his disciples gathered around him, and he began to teach them: How blest are the poor in spirit the reign of God is theirs. Blest too are the sorrowing; they shall be consoled. Blest are the lowly; they shall inherit the land. Blest are they who hunger and thirst for holiness; they shall have their fill. Blest are they who show mercy; mercy shall be theirs. Blest are the single-hearted for they shall see God. Blest too the peacemakers; they shall be called sons of God. Blest are those persecuted for holiness sake; the reign of God is theirs. Blest are you when they insult you and persecute you and utter every kind of slander against you because of me. Be glad and rejoice, for your reward is great in heaven; They persecuted the prophets before you the very same way."

Matthew 5.1-12.4.

After this reading, family members began to recall some past memories. They shared in a tearful way the hope to see their father again as he was before all the suffering. I mentioned to them that this reading from Matthew was really like Jesus inaugural address. It put forth the standards of the Kingdom and Jesus' ministry.

As Jesus initiated a theme for his ministry and his life, so, too, do we imitate Him in our own lives. It was a revelatory moment as we talked about the themes of kindness and gentleness in William's life. In using the scriptures to reflect on a person's life, the family sought to examine his life in light of the imperatives of the Kingdom. By doing so they broadened their perspective of grief and the nature of eternity. Such an exercise couldn't help but become internalized into self examination and transformation.

Our experience of death is in this instance a moment that will transform and allow us to gain a better awareness of where we are on our journey toward the Kingdom. Gathering together in preparing for the expression of faith at liturgical moments is a time of grace. Revelation and awareness of the mystery of life can be explored when Christians gather in this way. It bridges our feelings of loneliness, sorrow, and suffering by connecting us with those whom we love in the present and whom we will be with according to our hopes and prayers in eternity.

Pastoral Action

Meeting with this family was a pastoral action that I have always felt was very rewarding. Sometimes we realize in ministry that we receive blessings as we reach out to others. When I visited the house, I noticed the chair where William, as the 'patriarch' of the family, always sat. Sometimes those who have died are more present to us in death than they were in life. Suddenly, according to the psychology of death, we remember events, or a gesture, or something that they said. It may have seemed inconsequential in the past. It now takes on new meaning and they are very present in our minds. When I first looked at his chair, a flood of memories came over me. It was a gift of experiencing in my mind his presence in a special way. I knew him well in life from my visits and now I was remembering him at this time. His widow took the chair for herself. It was a silent transition for her, realizing that he no longer would be physically there with her.

When we meet with bereaved parishioners, they all have stories to tell us. In many ways they are doing spiritual grief work as they are beginning to establish a new relationship in faith. We must encourage stories and the use of the parishioners' imagination as they recall their loved one's presence. The pastoral preparation for the funeral is a significant ministry action that will contribute to healing for the bereaved.

Chapter Six

The Ritual's Biblical Roots

The Order of Christian Funerals is very much grounded in scripture. This chapter explores some of the biblical concepts that are prevalent and relate to the experience of loss. Becoming more familiar with biblical realities allows for better spiritual guidance for the grief-stricken.

A dynamic view of the Church and ministry emerges from the ritual. *The Order Of Christian Funerals* gives considerable attention to the reality and importance of scripture. We can reap considerable pastoral benefits by understanding biblical themes that are prevalent in the new rite.

The scriptures anchor pastoral activity both liturgically and pastorally. When we look at the themes emphasized in the *Order Of Christian Funerals*, our appreciation of grief and ministry can't help but be enhanced.

Scriptural categories relate to critical human situations. Bereavement understood as the reaction to the loss of a close relationship is very complex.[20] The human reaction and interaction with the mystery of God during bereavement deserves theological scrutiny. The biblical categories color the way we

---

20 Lawrence Boadt, Mary Dombeck, H. Richard Rutherford, *Rites of Death and Dying*, The Liturgical press, MN, 1998, p. 69

manage our grief. They are the very context for finding meaning and communion with those who have gone before us. Our faith response makes all the difference during bereavement. The beliefs we follow are the key for processing and accepting our feelings.

Exploring concepts such as the covenant, the new covenant, redemption, and community means journeying beyond our personal experiences. We have to keep in mind that "these concepts are language symbols which point beyond any one person's experience to the great mysteries of human existence."[21]

The biblical perspective allows us to envision mystery in reality through saving events. In the work entitled *The Book of the Acts of God*, G. Ernest Wright and Reginald H. Fuller make an important observation regarding the way we appreciate biblical events.

> In the Bible an important or signal happening is not an event unless it is also an event of revelation, that is, unless it is an event which has been interpreted so as to have meaning. Indeed, this is true for any fact. Unless it is given meaning in a certain context, it is meaningless and insignificant. Everything that is significant demands interpretation.[22]

Bereavement can be placed into a broad of context of meaning when associated with revelation. Biblical categories describe our relationship with God and one another. A pastoral scriptural concept found throughout the new rite is covenant. It is for

---

21 Homer Jernigan, "Toward a Theology of Peace," Boston University Papers, Boston, MA, p. 1

22 G. Ernest Wright & Reginald H. Fuller, *The Book of the Acts of God*, New York, Doubleday & Co., 1960, p.11

us, as it was for the Israelites, a concept through which we see all God's actions. It colors all we do and all we are. No longer can we experience death as final. We see death not as taking away but rather as change because we are in covenant both individually and as a community with God, who has broken the chains of bereavement. God has opened the vistas of life in covenant.

The Meaning of Covenant Especially for Grief

There are decisive moments in Israel's history of revelation. The Sinai Covenant expresses Israel's alliance with Yahweh.[23] Yahweh communicates the love, power, and fidelity which delivered Israel from Egyptian bondage. The tribal people who were elected by God's love are shaped by Him into a community with specific laws, worship, and a way of life. "I will be the God of all the tribes of Israel, and they shall be my people" (Jeremiah 31:1).

Yahweh initiates the covenant by an action called election.[24] Israel, by God's choice, becomes the people of Yahweh. This is an act of love (Deut.4:37) that gives us insight into the meaning of the event. The interpretation takes on a theological perspective of more than a treaty or contract in human terms. The formula clearly emphasizes that Israel has responsibilities and obligations because of its unique relationship with Yahweh. Being a loving election, this covenant goes beyond the understanding of the near Eastern contractual covenants that existed.

It is God who is acting in a loving way to assist and be present to Israelites. There is the promise of fulfillment evident

---

23 Rene Latourelle, S.J., *Theology of Revelation*, New York, Alba House, 1966, p.23

24 Raymond Brown, Joseph Fitzmeyer, Roland Murphy, eds. *The New Jerome Biblical Commentary*, New Jersey, Prentice Hall, 1990, 77:81, p.1298

in this relationship So, too, in our decisive moments is the need to live with promises and hope.

> You have seen what I did to the Egyptians, and how I bore you on eagles' wings and brought you to myself. Now therefore, if you will obey my voice and keep my covenant, you shall be my own possession among all peoples; for all the earth is mine, and you shall be to me a kingdom of priests and a holy nation.
>
> Exodus 19:4-6

The ministry of consolation in the *Order Of Christian Funerals* can best be implemented with solid notions of our covenantal bonding. The covenantal perspective of being empowered by God's love is the source of consolation for the bereaved. At the same time, it is the motivation for those who minister to the bereaved. Comforting the bereaved necessitates a theological frame work for ministry.

In order to minister to the bereaved, we must become familiar with a broader perspective. To just be there is not enough. Through kindness, through concern, and through knowledge of what the covenant means in our lives, the caregiver helps the bereaved to process the grief.

Within the covenantal relationship, there are important concepts that deepened and intensified the meaning of covenant, which gave the Israelite covenant a unique place among the cultures of its day. The Hebrew word for covenantal love is *hesed*. The New Jerome Biblical Commentary makes an interesting observation regarding the translation of the word.

The translation is defective in it's failure to indicate that *hesed* is not only the love exhibited in virtue of the covenant but also the movement of the will that initiates the covenant. In common usage *hesed* includes kinship love as well as covenant love.[25]

Hesed is a loving kindness, which, for the community, entails going beyond a minimal response. It is more than general kindness and concern. It is akin to being empathic and experiencing the feelings of others. Experiencing this love focuses the feelings into the relationship. This is a significant aspect of covenant for a theology of bereavement. This way of appreciating love is the dynamic active power for the community's life.

Covenantal love energizes those who are lacking strength due to losses. It is love that enables the bereaved to reinvest in relationships with others. Loving kindness empowers the bereaved to recognize that all bonds are not severed by death. The only real separation is being outside of the covenant. This certainly assists the bereaved in the necessary action of accepting a new spiritual relationship with the deceased loved one.

The theme of changing bonds is clearly evident in the new ritual's first liturgical prayers at the vigil for the deceased when the family and friends are invited to pray:

My brothers and sisters, we believe that all ties of friendship and affection which knit us as one throughout our lives do not unravel with death.

(*Order Of Christian Funerals,* par. 71)

---

25 Ibid., 77:95, p. 1298

The Old Testament Covenant was for Israel the beginning of all religious thought.[26] The covenantal relationship colors everything about the community's life and struggle. The image of God being with the people is experienced by ritualizing the covenant reality. The aspects of trust, fidelity, hope, and love are filtered through the covenantal experience. This relates to the way Israelites communicated with God and among themselves. Covenant theology is evident in the Book of Psalms. The presence of God and the poetic metaphors found in the psalms addresses bereavement within the covenantal relationship. Hebrew anthropology also plays a vital role in biblical theology and spirituality. When we examine biblical ideas about being a human person, our perspective about life and death is broadened. At the same time our appreciation of our relationship to God is expanded. There is a powerful impact to interpreting scripture, especially as we interpret it in light of our own experiences of bereavement.

The Psalms Especially for Bereavement

In addition to covenant, there are themes utilized within the ritual that deepen our understanding while assisting us in placing bereavement in a broader context. With the psalms we find a rich tapestry of feelings put into the wider perspective of covenanting with God's loving kindness in response to human feelings.

The Book of Psalms unveils many ways to communicate with God. Our whole heart can converse with God in a poetic

---

26 Joseph Komonchek, Mary Collins, Dermot Lane, *The New Theological Dictionary*, Wilmington, Del., Michael Glazier, 1987, p.244.

way through the hymn book of the Temple. The content of the revelation in the psalms provides us with many ways of expressing our innermost feelings. Feelings of separation and loss are released when the Psalmist praises the Lord in a variety of literary forms.

A spirituality for the bereaved may be developed through exploration of the psalms. The *Order Of Christian Funerals* gives attention to the importance of the psalms for the believing community. [27]

The psalms express the suffering and pain connected with loss; they relate to the need to trust in God for peace (*shalom*). The Psalmist converses with God, expressing deep feelings of anger, abandonment, weakness, and the hope for assistance. A journey into the Book of Psalms can help the bereaved to dialog with God about the loss.

The imagery, symbolism, and metaphors in the psalms contribute to the theology of bereavement a theology that is far more experiential than systematic. The theological concepts in the psalms speak to the immediate concrete experience of loss.

> I am weary with crying my throat is parched my eyes grow dim with waiting for my God.
>
> Ps.69:3

In the psalms we find the empowering action of God grasping us in our emptiness. Real peace is provided in the psalms. It is a way of going through the process and realizing the presence of the Lord.

---

[27] I.C.E.L. *Order of Christian Funerals,* Chicago, Liturgy Training Publications, 198, par.244.

> "I waited patiently for the Lord, he inclined to me and heard my cry, He drew me up from the desolate pit, out of the miry bog, and set my feet upon a rock, making my steps secure."
>
> Ps.40:1-2

There is the covenantal relationship in the psalms. Psalm 81 illustrates the Covenantal renewal. Other appropriate Covenant Psalms are Ps.78, 89,132.[28] In the psalms we experience Yahweh's saving intervention. It is Yahweh who communicates with our hearts.

Wholeness of heart is an important theme to explore for insights into bereavement. Hans Joachim Kraus commented on the wholeness of life. His words give us insight into wholeness, which is meaningful for our relationship with God and one another, especially while grieving or ministering to those who grieve.

> In the relationship of life and death this finds expression once more. The sorrowing person has a "broken heart" (Ps.34:18; 51:17;102:4 109:22143:4;147:3).His heart has become like wax melted within him (Ps.22:14). The center of human existence has collapsed and dissolved. In view of this weakening and dissolving of life at its center, it is the wish of everyone who has experienced Yahweh's saving intervention, "May your hearts live for ever!"(Ps.22:26). Both the body and the heart fail (Ps.73:26) but the hearts of those who seek God can revive (Ps.69:32).[29]

---

[28] Bernhard W. Anderson, *Out of the Depths, The Psalms Speak for Us Today*, Philadelphia, The Westminster Press, 1983, p.237

[29] Hans–Joachim Kraus, *Theology of the Psalms,* Min., Augsburg Publishing Co., 1986, p.146

The Lament psalms describe feelings related to grieving. We may feel sick or grieve losses in life in a wider context of meaning (Ps. 6:2; 13:3; 22:14-15; 38:5-6; 39:4-6).The psalms relate to our distress and provide rich poetic forms of expression.

"For my life is spent with grief and my years with sighing; My strength has failed through affliction, and my bones are consumed."

(Ps.31.10)

The reality of death is felt throughout the Psalter (Ps. 28:1; 59:3; 88:3-9). This aspect of separation is woven throughout the psalms. As the people's liturgical hymn book, the psalms provide us with a way of expressing our longings in a ritually fulfilling way. Creative power and hope in God are clearly found in the psalms (Ps.139; 62; 16; 27; 65; 23; 121) The disharmonious aspects of life are not denied. There is a rich awareness of our fragmentation, which is put into the dialogue with God.

Bereavement necessitates redefining our relationship with the deceased. Also, there may well be a need to redefine our relationship with God.[30] The psalms facilitate spiritual growth as they give us permission to express our real feelings of grieving with God. Anger, abandonment, emptiness, and longing are some of the emotions found in the psalms of Lament. They go beyond just receiving permission to express ourselves. They connect us with the eternal now, where all things are renewed. The psalms allow us to not only touch the heart of God and His loving kindness,

---

30 Therese Rando, *Clinical Interventions for Caregivers*, Illinois, Research Press Co., 1984, p.101

but they also put us in touch with His loving kindness. In a deep, faith-filled way, we know that there is more than death.

Creation and Chaos

Another important biblical theme that relates to grieving is creation. The loss of a close relationship can be a shattering experience. The chaos and the void in a great abyss are biblical descriptions that are applicable to our experience in the crisis.

The experience of intense grief is manifested by disorganization. There is a need to be empowered and creatively proceed toward reorganizing our lives. The shared effort in ministry among the members of the community facilitating creative power for the bereaved is an action of continual creation.

Being with the bereaved means cooperating with creative power. It is choosing life and helping those who experience death to pass through the darkness to light.

The accounts of the Israelites wandering in the desert and searching for direction provides insight to grieving The Israelite desert experience is the situation when revelation occurred. Amidst the existential emptiness, spiritual growth is possible. The experience of loss is an experience of needing to cope, to express the loss through grieving, and hopefully to reorganize our lives to spiritually grow.

The Israelite history is a history of broken relationships in the covenant. What appeared to be meaningful and good was only an appearance. The false idols did not bring fulfillment to the community's life. Another theological lesson can be taught about grieving in this context. Amidst the pain there can be an embracing of idols. There are many ways that this is possible in our culture. The bereaved may find chemical dependency in drugs and alcohol as an example of idolatry in grieving. Promiscuity in sexual relationships may be sought as avoidance or denial for losses. It is here that we rage at life by destroying all that we hold dear. As the Israelites forgot their relationship with God, as they danced before the golden calf, so, too, may the bereaved create similar idols in unhealthy relationships and escapes.

New Covenant Relationship

The prophet Jeremiah (31:31-34) made known for the people the establishment of a new covenant. Here again the important image of the heart is used by a biblical personality:

> The days are coming, says the Lord, when I will make a new covenant with the house of Israel and the house of Judah. It will not be Like the covenant I made with their fathers the day I took them by the hand to lead them forth from the land of Egypt, for they broke my covenant and I had to show myself their master, says the Lord. But this is the covenant which I will make with the house of Israel after those days, says the Lord. I will place my law within them and write it upon their hearts; I will be their God, and they shall be my people.
>
> (Jer.31:31-34)

The early Christians regarded themselves as bound together by covenant. The covenant in the New Testament is a "most free, creative reinterpretation of the older traditions."[31]

---

31 *Interpreter's Dictionary of the Bible*, Vol.1, Nashville, Abingdon Press, 1979, p.160

The narratives of the Last Supper are the primary source (Matt. 26:28; Mark 14:24; Luke22:20; 1Cor.11:25). The New Covenant institution and the Exodus event (24:8) are connected as free actions of God's love, establishing an even deeper relationship of intimacy. The New Covenant fulfills both the Old one and the words of the prophets.

The New Covenant is by its very nature communal. In the Eucharist there is the expression of fellowship or participation (2 Cor.13:14; Phil.2:1) in the Spirit. The community becomes the agency by the which the Spirit works in the world. The Incarnate presence of Christ is continued in the community of faith. There is a continual creation, especially in ways of bringing consolation to those experiencing chaos through the loss of a loved one.

The community continues the ministry of reconciliation (2Cor.5:18) in Christ. The ministry of consolation is an aspect of that same ministry. This shalom is to be experienced within the community of faith. The Spirit empowers the community to bring peace to each other in critical moments. Consolation means to act in a way that brings comfort or peace.

The Body of Christ

Paul uses the metaphor of the body to express community life (Col.2:18, 19). The Spirit brings peace and intimacy to the relationship with God. Pauline writings (Rom. 8:15) express an intimacy with God according to the creative presence of the Spirit, which renews the face of the earth.

A spiritual response to bereavement looks to the working of the Holy Spirit in the life of a Christian. The receiving of the Spirit in baptism initiates the Christian's journey toward the

Kingdom. In infant baptism, the candidate is carried into the assembly to share in the mysteries of faith and the reception of the Spirit. Baptism happens to the person within the community. It does not happen apart from the community. The community as an entity welcomes the new member to share in its faith response to God. This invitation is to participate in God's saving actions to be one of His chosen people, a royal priesthood and a people set apart by God s love.

The experience of saving signs has to be appreciated as an event that happens, not to the individual apart, but rather immersed in the community. So, too, it is when the Christian's body is carried into the assembly for the funeral. The signs and symbols, such as the white pall and the as sprinkling of water, point toward baptism. They are reminders of the Christian life we have led as members of the People of God.

The Easter symbol of the paschal candle illustrates not only our death and resurrection in Christ but also the flame of faith that symbolizes our hope for the return in glory at the Second Coming. The Eucharist in this context is appreciated as the mystery of faith. Our participation is within the symbol of the covenant reality.

The communal aspect of faith is critical for a theology of bereavement. Our connectedness brings about healing from our feelings of abandonment, isolation, and possibly estrangement. Spiritual growth occurs within the covenantal bonding of love (agape), which seals our relationship as a community.

Biblical faith in the context of bereavement takes on a rich interpretation of what it means to have and to be a community of believers. The healing necessary to go through the darkness of grief is present among the community of believers. The more expansive concepts of life, covenant, creation, and expression are present for the bereaved.

Bereavement marks the time we as mortals stand on the edge of our worldly experiences and look beyond the horizon to eternity. Not only do we experience crushing loss, we also begin to see there is more than just this. We realize death is just the limit of our sight there is much more. The limitations of our seeing are corrected by our faith relationship with God. When we walk by faith, the horizon is limitless.

While we continue to only see through the glass darkly, we realize in Pauline thought that we are still members in the Body. Our ability to redefine our relationships is possible in a covenantal perspective.

A spirituality for bereavement seeks to capture the concepts and perspective woven throughout the ritual to broaden our outlook. This puts the loss, however great it may be, into the wider reality of Christian faith and covenant. While the grief continues, it is carried through the care of the loving community. No longer can grief be interpreted as a crushing burden. It is more than that for the Christian. It is an opportunity to grow spiritually, and, by so doing, change our hearts both individually and collectively. As our hearts are torn up by the roots, we come to realize that the wellspring of our faith is something physical reality cannot take from us. Christ is the eternal offering of God, who comforts us through His people.

Bereavement is a time when ultimate questions are asked about our existence.[32] It is important to explore those questions. The best way to question and seek meaning is within the context

---

[32] Charles Gerkin, *Crisis Experience in Modern Life, Theory and Theology for Pastoral Care*, Nashville, Abingdon Press, 1979, p.160

of a caring community. The community of faith provides ways to ritualize our losses and at the same time explore our ultimate concerns.

Thomas, the doubter, confronted with the death of his friend, couldn't believe in anything. Amidst his terrible, hollow grief, he stayed with the community. They sustained him until he could believe when his friend and Lord appeared. While Thomas received the ultimate grace of seeing the Risen Lord, the Lord looked to us and said, "Blessed are they who believe and do not (yet) see."

When there is the gathering together in the Christian assembly, there is the remembering of God's relationship in Christ. This kind of ongoing memorial is the biblical re-presenting of a saving action. The Passover meal was for the Israelites an action of God liberating them from bondage in the present. The Exodus was re-enacted in the present. In the Eucharist, our memorial, the entire Church both the living and the dead comes together in the Spirit. We are closer and bonded with our loved ones. This is a liberating action from the bondage of grieving.

The existential here and now of worship recreates and re-enacts our relationship with God. The communion of saints is put into its proper perspective as participating in the selfsame Spirit as the believing community. Our covenant cleanses us of idolatrous approaches and points toward the oneness with God and those who have journeyed before us in faith. Together we await the return of the Lord.

While we wait, we celebrate festivals of faith. The festivals are ones of remembrance. The celebrations of liturgies in the Christian community reflect our oneness in Christ. We are empowered by this connectedness in the Body of Christ. This empowering presence is the source of healing and reconciliation.

The biblical perspective provides us with ways to pastorally reach out, preach, and teach the bereaved. The scriptures are the resource for the Christian community. Our dialogue with God is deepened as we explore revelation, especially during our experience of loss. The experience of loss in the Christian community is an opportunity for spiritual growth. It is a time when we can open ourselves to ponder realities. Grief can be a graced moment for the bereaved. While we suffer and cry, we, through the outreach of others who share our faith, can begin to see beyond the loss to the bright, new hope for the eternal Jerusalem of the People of God. We are graced to accept the loss, allow God's People to help, and reorganize our lives in light of our faith individually and as a community member.

Biblical reflection focuses our faith and good works. This pastoral approach allows the time for the faith of the community, which too often lies dormant, to break forth into ministry. It is a harnessing of the community's faith, focusing it on the bereaved and the unfolding of that faith into the helping action of the community.

The ministry of consolation, for many, becomes and remains a graced moment of God touching us both as individuals and as a community to help, to teach, and most of all to heal those in need.

This growth touches all who minister to the needs of the bereaved. When the parish initiates an outlook for bereavement, the ministry can develop. This development is the expression of a compassionate and loving community. This is in keeping with the word of God, who forms us and calls us to minister to each other.

Pastoral Action

Pastoral care is rooted in the scriptures. The biblical categories provide us with frameworks for expressing ourselves in the context of faith. The Psalms were the prayers Jesus prayed. When we pray as Jesus did we join our suffering to His. The Psalms unlock for us our feelings, especially as we cry out to God. The poetic images give us ways to really be expressive with our feelings. It is always important, whether pastorally caring at a retreat or day of recollection, along with major liturgies to include Psalms. They really are cries of the heart.

We need to deepen our relationship with God, especially while we grieve. It is a time of deep trouble and chaos for many people. Our approach to scripture has to be pastoral and personal. If we can help the bereaved to express their loss through the catalyst of the Word in scripture, these categories of chaos, creation, covenant, and the Psalms will take on new meaning as we pastorally explore the text and their underlying meaning for our lives.

Chapter Seven

Children and Loss

This chapter highlights certain aspects of grief that surround the loss of a child: the ritual aspects of the loss of an infant, parental grief, discussing death with children, children and funerals, and the Order of Christian Funerals for Children

Certain circumstances such as miscarriages, stillbirths, and infant deaths require some very careful pastoral planning. Helping and healing for those suffering the loss of a child is one of the most difficult tasks confronting every parish community.[33]

The death of a child is a crisis that deeply affects people's lives. The pain from such loss defies description. According to the *New England Journal of Medicine,* approximately 31 percent of all pregnancies end in miscarriage.[34] Yet our culture does not always recognize this loss. Couples silently grieve this death of a dream for a new infant family member. The pastoral response has to be immediate and empathic. The more time elapses before pastoral intervention, the less effective is the way the bereaved manage their grief.

---

33 Victor M. Parachim, "Helping Families Survive Stillbirth, Providing Pastoral Care When Nothing Feels Real Except The Pain," *The Priest,* May 1991, Vol. 47, No.5, pp. 18-20

34 Dena Salmon, "Coping With Miscarriage," *Parent*, May 1991, p.110

The *Order of Christian Funerals* is a healing vehicle for expressing the hurt and pain. The ritual offers a way to mourn with the help of family and friends. The funeral liturgy establishes the baby as a person who was part of a family. In light of the ritual, families are encouraged to have a funeral.

Recently, a couple in our parish experienced a miscarriage. I met with them as soon as possible. The pastoral meeting took on remarkable significance concerning arrangements. At first the mother, Susan, thought that I would meet her and her husband, Carl, at the cemetery for a few prayers at the grave. After I spoke with the couple, deep feelings came to light.

Susan and Carl thought that the burial would take place earlier in the day. When I was to offer the prayers, there would only be some flowers and the noticeable space on the ground where the small while coffin was to be buried. Plans changed as we talked.

The couple had viewed the infant's body and was aware of the way the coffin would look. A prayer service according to the ritual was explained and took place.

The "Rite of Final Commendation for an Infant" (O.C.F. par. 318) is recommended when an infant is stillborn or a newborn dies. This ritual ought to be made available for miscarriages as well.[35]

This can take place at a hospital or place of birth, church, funeral home, or their own home at the time of the committal. If they want a mass, that, too could be arranged with permission at some other suitable place. The ritual clearly states that the prayer service is a model. The minister ought to adapt it to circumstances.

---

35 Terence Curley, "When A Child Dies," *Celebration*, Vol.22, No.11, Nov. 1993, pp.438-440

Before the funeral, another pastoral concern connected with grief ought to be explored. The name of the child is very significant for the family, both for the burial and later memories.

Naming the Infant

When asked whether the couple had "named" the baby, they told me his name was to be "Carl." It bothered them that even though the infant was baptized, no name was previously given at the time. I explained that the parents name the baby. This is in keeping with being co-creators. If they would like, the naming could be done before the funeral liturgies.

Naming the child who has died focuses the grief. The infant is not thought of in an impersonal manner. Naming also connects the grieving mother and father with the dreams they had for a child. The parent is better able to express the loss when it is made more personal. Along with this psychological awareness of the significance, naming connects the family with ways to remember the infant in faith.

At the funeral liturgies, we speak of the infant by name. Calling upon God in remembering this infant by name as one who is in the Kingdom is a more comforting prayer.

A Ritual for Naming

A ritual for naming an infant who died because of miscarriage or stillbirth does not have to be lengthy. Pastoral circumstances allow for many variations in the way it is conducted. A naming ritual may be modeled after the way an infant is presented for baptism. The ritual words may be adapted for a baptized or unbaptized child. This ritual is in keeping with the *Order of Christian Funeral*'s concern for the bereaved. Developing a ritual requires creative ministry for communicating healing and hope to the bereaved.

A sample approach may be the following:

Priest/Deacon:"What name did you give to your child?" (Name of Child) Priest/Deacon "You named your child, asking for faith and salvation in Jesus Christ. We now ask that we receive comfort consolation, knowing through faith that (Name of Child) is in the Kingdom of Heaven."

This rite may be adapted to the setting. When the couples are together with family and friends, it may be lengthened to include prayers of petition and an "Our Father."

The naming of the child ought to be done as soon as possible. It can take place in a hospital room, home, or church. We believe that life begins at conception. This life is precious in the eyes of the Lord. Our celebration of life in the Kingdom of Heaven is an act of love. This is another way the bereaved begin to accept the loss and place it into the context of religious faith.

Other questions were explored when we met. Susan was very open regarding her feelings of loss. Carl, her husband, although tearful, did not talk as much as she did. Both of them expressed intense disappointment.

The couple really had little warning; the medical reasons for the death were still inconclusive. The couple said they that they were willingly allowed an autopsy with the hope that it would help the medical profession to know more about infant death.

At our meeting, they expressed how they were shocked and saddened. They volunteered that they were angry and cried out to God. As the pastoral caregiver, it was necessary for me to let them know that these emotions were not unusual for this type of experience. God really does understand and is not upset with us when we cry out to Him like that. If anything, God, who is the God of all consolation, cries with us. When the pastoral caregiver gives permission for the bereaved to own their feelings and express them, real support and healing can occur.

Our response to this loss is best expressed by sharing with the bereaved a loving image of God. It is not the time to become philosophical or try to explain away God's will. Searching for answers, denial, and anger are very real characteristics associated with grief. Our role is to be a loving listener who helps release authentic feelings of loss.

Susan and Carl decided to have prayer services at the funeral home and cemetery. The entire family would be invited. I pointed out to them how not only their dream of this child was gone but other family members also felt the loss as well. They, too, needed to express this loss and comfort those who are suffering intense grief. The maternal and paternal grandparents were invited. Members of past generations were not offered this consolation. During these liturgies, grandparents often cry not only for the grandchild but for the child whom they lost many years before and were not able or allowed to express their grief over at that time. They truly understand and have compassion steeped in wisdom.

Suggestions were made regarding the liturgy. Susan and Carl were told how I'd seen other couples take part in liturgies for miscarriages of a stillborn infant. Sometimes a toy would be placed in the casket, or a poem or goodbye would be read by the parents. The placing of symbols or objects in the casket presumes that viewing is possible. Viewing the body is encouraged as another healing aspect for grief.

They were also told how couples decide to put their loving thoughts into words for the liturgy. Both agreed that this would be meaningful for them. After the liturgies, they let me take a copy of their goodbye with the thought that I could help other parents like them in the future. What this mother and father wrote provides insight to the grief and ways to express loss. It is a meaningful and moving tribute to the sanctity and love of life a parent has for an unborn child. At the same time, as sad and upsetting as it is to hear the words, we realize that healing is occurring.

A Mother's Grief

Every time I think about you, I want to cry.
Only because I don't have all the reasons why.
I remember the first time I felt you move.
I only wish your daddy could have felt it, too.
You gave us so much joy.
It's because all along we knew we were having
a little baby boy.
We love you and we will never forget you.

A Father's Grief

The first time we saw you on the ultrasound screen, we
Were so happy God gave you to us. We looked forward
to holding you all day and all night. And the days that came
to follow, to hear you cry at night, to know that you need us.

The night that I held you, I knew that I could not hold you ever again. You brought so much joy to me when you were here that I find it very hard to say good bye to my son, Carl. I love you very much. God look over our little angel.

In every rite of passage, there is meaning given to the celebration by our using words and gestures. The *Order of Christian Funerals* is sensitive to the healing that occurs when we ritualize. At the appropriate moment in planning the funeral liturgy, this special prayer from the ritual could be used. Later, when it is used in the rite, it will be remembered and can be a resource for healing. His prayer or one of our own assists the bereaved in ritualizing their loss.

Lord God, ever caring and gentle, we commit to your love this little one, quickened to life a short time. Enfold him/her in eternal life. We pray for his/her parents Who are saddened by the loss of their child. Give them courage and help them in their pain and grief. May they all meet one day. In the joy and peace of your kingdom. We ask this through Christ our Lord.

Amen. (*OCF*, par.399)

An infant's death is considered by clergy and people as a painful experience.[36] Our human expectations are geared toward happy endings. While the pain from such losses engenders pain, we cannot stop at that point. Our real interpretation of happiness is entrance into the Kingdom. We cannot leave people uncomforted or unable to grow through their losses. Ritual actions and prayers bring expression of loss, which leads

---

36 Richard J. Shmaruk, "One of Our Most Difficult Pastoral Moments," *The Priest*, June. 1992,Vol.48, No.6, p.13

the bereaved toward hope in the Kingdom. These rituals and others are meant to assist the bereaved parents in seeing beyond the limits imposed by grief. Out of the darkness, light and peace will prevail when we are together again in the Kingdom of Heaven.

Rituals and pastoral care have to connect in the parish community. The ministry of consolation in a parish may include those who have suffered losses. They who have gone through similar suffering are the best caregivers. Once they have had time to adjust, they can be helped further by visiting and helping others.

In the *Order of Christian Funerals* (par. 240), the ritual recommends inviting members of the community who have lost children to help families in their struggle to accept the loss of their child. This is a very healthy and therapeutic ministry for everyone concerned. Parish support groups for losses at various times in the lifecycle bring considerable healing. They are also a resource for the ministry of consolation.

Once someone has been sufficiently helped with managing their loss, they can become a pastoral visitor to others. Pastoral visitors reach out to those special circumstances of loss. "Ended Beginnings Groups" or "Compassionate Friends" may volunteer to visit families suffering grief from miscarriages, stillbirths, or infant death. They can help with questions about how to cope with the loss. When someone has experienced such a loss, they can often help with questions regarding siblings or other children's reactions to it. They are aware of the strain the death places on the entire family. Many times the presence of a pastoral visitor comes at a time when reassurance is necessary.

Discussing Death with Children

The way a child experiences loss cannot be overlooked. When a death occurs in a family, very often children are not included. They are overlooked as persons who grieve. More information about how children grieve is necessary for pastoral caregivers.

There are difficulties in knowing how to communicate with the young child about the death of a sibling, classmate, or relative, such as an aunt, uncle, grandparent, and even a parent. Mr. Rogers of *Mister Roger's Neighborhood* produced a pamphlet about talking with young children regarding death.[37] Mr. Rogers, whom we think of as a children's show host, was also ordained as a Presbyterian minister. In his work with children, he noted that feelings of exclusion are far more detrimental for the child than feelings of sadness. They may even blame themselves for the death, or misinterpret the event in other ways. The child may become anxious. In other words, adults have to be careful not to project on children their own denial by avoiding the topic.

A child's view of death is a product of the imagination and fantasy of childhood. Mr. Rogers explained death by describing the loss that the child may identify within his/her world. The "death of a goldfish" helps the child to associate that death with others. Children interpret death literally Mistakes are made when a child is told that someone has "gone away" or are "asleep." They simply wonder when the person will return or wake up. Using euphemisms with children (as with adults)

---

[37] Fred Rogers, *Talking With Young Children About Death*, Family Communications, Inc., Pittsburgh, PA, 1979

really is not a good idea. It only confuses the way to relate to and accept death. Another very important aspect of death is how God is involved in it for the child.

There are major difficulties in this regard if we do not present God correctly when we talk about death.[38] When a child is told that someone was so good God took him/her, then difficulties are sure to follow. The child thinks, *If I am really good, then God will take me, too."* This is an alarming thought for a child.

We have to be aware of children's casual connections. The term "magical thinking" refers to a child's way of knowing applied to death. For example, a child may feel instrumental in a death. Grandma may have died and the child remembers that he did not give her a kiss the last time they met. Somehow children attribute how they feel or think as the cause for the death.[39] The family and pastoral caregiver have to help the child realize that it is one thing to feel a certain way and something else to cause a physical event.

Magical thinking relates to the child's image of God. Studies have been done as to how children imagine what God is like God is a protector and a loving friend with exceptional powers.[40] God can similarly be feared as the one who takes people we love away from us. In describing the death of a loved one to a child, natural causes ought to be explained. It is far better to say that a grandparent had a sick heart that could not go on working. The weakness of the muscles caused it to stop and he/she died.

---

38 Terence Curley, "Pastoral Care and the Child's Experience of Loss," *The Priest*, May 1992, Vol.48, No. 5, p.36

39 Therese Rando, *Grief, Dying, and Death, Clinical Interventions for Caregivers*, Research Press Co., Illinois, 1984, pp.166-172

40 Ibid, p.168

Children and Funeral Attendance

Parents at the time of a death find themselves in a very difficult position. They are faced with the question of whether their child should attend the wake and funeral. They are torn between knowledge that acceptance of death is necessary and wanting to protect the child. Decisions about whether the child ought to attend the funeral are difficult to determine.

Children should be given the opportunity to whether or not to attend the funeral..If they decide not to go, that decision should be respected. They should be told that they may visit the grave or the church when they want to, with the accompaniment of an adult if they desire. If they decide to go, the details should be explained in advance so that they will have some idea of what to expect. [41]

Children should not be forced to attend the funeral. They can visit the grave at another time. In the movie *My Girl*, insights to a child's perception of loss are treated in a loving and compassionate way. One scene is when young Veda leaves her room, deciding to go downstairs in the family funeral home to see her childhood friend. The reality of loss and the need for help and understanding is depicted as she flees to her teacher.

Towards the end of the movie, Veda reads a poem about her grief to the creative writing class. The poem ritualizes her loss and helps her to accept the death. Children, like adults, need to ritualize in age-appropriate ways. Very often, drawing

---

[41] Earl A. Grollman, *Concerning Death A Practical Guide For The Living*, Beacon Press, Boston, MA, 1974, pp. 65-80

pictures or writing down prayers and letters are ways to work through the loss. This movie is a fine example of a production that can help young children, probably from ten or eleven years, to accept the reality of loss. The younger child would be best helped by attending this movie with an adult. This would ensure that both could talk about it in a beneficial way.

Some parish schools of religious formation have prayer services for children and their losses. The services can include brothers, sisters, parents, grandparents, cousins, aunts, uncles, playmates, or classmates in the prayers. [42]

Some Concluding Ideas for Pastoral Action with Children's Grief

1. Talk with the child in age-appropriate ways. Try to realize what he/she is able to understand.
2. Let the child know precisely what happened. This means explaining what happened according to natural causes.
3. Be aware of the child's lack of expression in grief. He/she may know but not show he/she feels.
4. Reassure them of your love and their goodness.
5. Don't be alarmed if they "play" funeral. Playing is the child's way of working things out.
6. The child may idealize or imitate the decease. This is similar to an adult symptom, which is normal.
7. Help the child express feelings. Art expresses both cognitive and emotional awareness.

---

[42] Terence Curley, *The Ministry of Consolers*, The Liturgical Press, Collegeville, MN, 2004, chapter 4, "The Grief Minister and the Grieving Child."

8. Invite the child to the wake (vigil) and funeral. Look for resistance and explore the reasons with the child.
9. Explain the religious significance of being on a journey toward the Kingdom of God. In age-appropriate ways, explain that even Jesus had to suffer because of the love God has for us.
10. Explain that there are ways we can remember the person who died. Praying in an informal way and encouraging the child to pray on his/her own for the loved one is a healthy spirituality for grief.

Chapter Eight

The Church's Prayer for Healing and Hope

The Office as the ancient prayer of the Church with scripture and Psalms brings healing and hope to the bereaved. In the Office for the Dead there is a way of placing loss into the context of faith provided in the Order of Christian Funerals. This chapter explores this option from the ritual for the believing community.

In life, faith responses have to be rooted in a deep and abiding awareness that what we do is done in the presence of God. This is especially pertinent during bereavement. At times of separation and loss we need to be connected with the community of faith, worshiping and assisting one another in ways that bring healing and hope.

In our society it is necessary that we have a better awareness as to how to respond to loss. We live in a world that denies death and subsequent grief. In this setting, the Church is challenged to bring healing. Our grief can only be complicated by denial of life's losses. Such denial brings further obstacles into our lives.

Our losses have to be placed into a context that provides meaning and ways to sort things out amidst all of the chaos. This context is the context of faith. Religious faith provides a dimension of meaning not found anywhere else. Faith informs us about our lives and how ultimate they are in light of eternity.

There is a certain peace and acceptance offered in Christian communities doing acts of worship.

The *Order of Christian Funerals* provides a variety of options that relate to times of loss. The ritual actions and prayers are illuminating and healing for all who are so affected by our culture of disbelief and denial.

Prayers, psalms, and readings are included in the ritual. This is markedly different from past rituals, which often made only references. What is wonderfully included are morning and evening prayers from the *Office for the Dead*. This chapter will focus on the importance of this inclusion in the ritual. While there are other options in the ritual, this one has remarkable ramifications for the real meaning of the community coming together to express grief. The *Liturgy of the Hours* in this context communicates our very identity as an ecclesial community.

Ecclesial Prayer For Those Who Died

Ministry and participation are continually emphasized as we read the instructions according to the ritual. The gather together or "ecclesia" has the rich tradition of praying for one another from the very beginning of the Church. The early community at Jerusalem as portrayed in the *Acts of the Apostles* introduces liturgies of prayer that prefigured the *Liturgy of the Hours*.

The importance of communal prayer sets the tone for the *Order of Christian Funerals*. We find in the ritual's general introduction St. Paul's letter to the early church at Corinth. "If one member of the body of Christ, which is the Church, suffers, all members suffer with that member" (1 Corinthians 12:26).

Even though grief has some intensely private aspects to it, it cannot be solely experienced in that way by the Christian. The community is called to prayer when a member dies. At the same time, we are instructed to console one another with our faith.

We pray in imitation of Christ as one community of believers gathering together in faith. This includes those who are grieving, pastoral caregivers and members of the parish wanting to console coming together at specific times for support. This gathering together is sacramental and signifies the hope that in the presence of God we can have our grief convert into grace. This grace will empower us to continue on the journey, not forgetting members who have gone before us in faith.

Paul's Letter to the Hebrews gives us a model for praying in imitation of Christ. "In the days when he was in the flesh, he offered prayers and supplications with loud cries and tears to God, who was able to save him from death, and he was heard because of his reverence. (Hb.5:7).

Emptying ourselves is detaching and letting go, not into an abyss, but rather letting go of destructive emotions and connecting in faith to a relationship. This new relationship possible through communal prayer is with God, our loved one who has died, and all those we journey with as we live our lives with new meaning given to life's separations and losses. As Jesus emptied himself to the Father, so, too, we, as members of His Church, imitate this saving action in our prayers.

To Pray As Jesus Did

The Psalter is our rich resource in faith for ways to praise God even while we are lamenting. We are very much in imitation of the Lord when we worship and pray the Psalms. The Psalms give us spiritual guidance for our converse with the Father. While we console others, we are enriched in our ministry by the Psalms.

Gathering together to pray the *Office for the Dead* is "to offer praise and thanks to God especially for the gifts of redemption and resurrection, to intercede for the dead, and to find strength in Christ's victory over death." While praying the ritual, we find that the prayers further elaborate that Christ is truly present through the Holy Spirit in the gathered assembly of faith. In our rich traditions of faith, the invitation to pray the Psalms is extended to us in communion with those who have always, throughout the ages, prayed the Psalms.

Instruction Necessary

Celebrating the *Office for the Dead* requires preparation. The ritual emphasizes the need for pastors and other ministers to provide catechesis on the purpose, place, and significance of the *Liturgy of the Hours* as they are expressed in the *Office for the Dead*. Members of the parish community are to be encouraged to participate, which will support and be a sign of faith in the Paschal Mystery.[43]

There are a number of places where the *Office for the Dead* may be celebrated. In many instances we are seeing that Catholics are becoming aware of the option to celebrate the vigil in the parish church. The vigil in itself, when celebrated, is the first liturgical moment in the funeral journey. It certainly is

---

43 Terence Curley, "Catechesis for Those Who Mourn," *The Priest*, Vol.57, No. 3, March 2001, p.35

more solemn and respectful when we celebrate this in the parish church. The sense of the sacred is not always upheld in the secular setting of the funeral parlor. Praying the psalms in the presence of the Lord in the church's special environment is a more encompassing spiritual atmosphere.

The parish is the suitable place for Christians to go through grief. In fact, given our culture of denial, the parish is extraordinarily appropriate for the grief stricken to come to terms with their loss in the consoling presence of the Lord. They can look upon their loved one as resting in the Lord. Again, this is not anywhere as apparent in the funeral home. Consequently, when parishes offer the option of having the vigil replacing the funeral home "wake," more and more parishioners opt for this for their loved ones when they participate in the parish setting.

Long after the funeral is over, parish liturgies, support groups, and pastoral visits will all complement the care expressed at the time of the funeral. We have to keep in mind that the psalms are especially meant to be expressed in song. The cantor and other members of the music ministry can far more effectively celebrate the vigil in this setting over the secular ones.

The *Order of Christian Funerals* includes both "morning prayer" and "evening prayer." This develops ways to take the journey in faith begun in baptism by the deceased Christian. Now, we fill the final part of the journey with prayer in the hope for the deceased to cross over the waters of death and enter eternal life. These prayers may be offered within the vigil and on the day of the funeral (usually in the morning).[44]

---

44 Terence Curley, "The Office for the Dead: A Parish Prayer," *The Priest*, Vol.52, No.11, Nov. 1996, p.12

There is real flexibility for parishes as to the times when the *Office* may be prayed. Parishes may schedule the *Office for the Dead* according to their own customs. Special liturgical times such as Advent, Lent, and remembrances during November as the Month of All Souls are meaningful and consoling celebrations. Our hope is to find in breaking open the word a consolation we can only receive from our loving God, who promises eternal life for ourselves and those who have gone before us in faith.

Spiritual Relationship

The most significant task of grief work is to develop a new relationship in faith with loved ones who have died. Good grief work entails letting go of the physical presence and welcoming a new spiritual way of relating. Faith informs and promises that we will be together again in the heavenly reunion. This purpose and interpretation to our losses far surpasses the merely human ways of trying to cope. We realize through revelation that this spiritual way of coping brings consolation as we continue in a hope-filled way our earthly journey.

Morning Prayer

Let us explore some aspects of the way the *Office* brings hope and consolation. In the *Morning Prayer,* the assembly recalls the power of the resurrection. It reminds us of Christ's victory over death. This gathering together facilitates healing for the bereaved. The ritual confronts loss and reduces the possibility of denial. When we begin to experience our loss in the context of faith, we are better equipped to accept. The hope is that the more we pray, the more we learn to trust and love again.

When circumstances change, other Psalms may be used that are more suitable for new occurrences. When parishes go through a preparation for the *Office for the Dead,* the community is more aware of how this relates to their needs, both spiritual and emotional, during times of loss. Through homilies, parish support groups, grief seminars, and other pastoral ways, this may be accomplished.

The structure and the readings for *Morning Prayer* are available in the instruction. What may be added is an explanation of the readings, which may assist the bereaved in placing the loss into the context of faith. Through reflections, new insights about grief are given.

An example of a brief interpretation about what it means to "praise God by way of lamenting" gives the bereaved permission to authentically express their feelings of loss. Pastoral leaders ought not to be disturbed by hearing people cry. This is a healthy and healing aspect of liturgy. The emotional expression is a catharsis and a necessary release for the grief-stricken.

Evening Prayer

Evening Prayer is similar in structure to *Morning Prayer.* The overall themes are the remembering of Christ's sacrifice and the saving works of redemption. The community throughout the liturgy thanks God for the gift of life given to the deceased Christian. There is then a remembering concerning the Christian as being part of creation. At both the *Morning* and the *Evening Prayers,* there is a time for a farewell proclaimed by a family member or friend.

The *Farewell* in the funeral liturgy at the vigil, at the *Office for the Dead,* or at the *Funeral Mass* is not a eulogy. It is rather a celebration of the Christian's accomplishments in him/her by our loving God. When the *Farewell* is offered in the context of faith at an appropriate time, it is an expression of God's redemptive love for the deceased and their good works.

Ministry Points for Pondering

1. Through scripture seminars or parish workshops, we can inform parishioners abut the importance of praying the *Liturgy of the Hours.*
2. The parish newsletter, bulletins, and evenings of explanation may be offered to familiarize parishioners with the *Office.*
3. Establish liturgical feasts or time in the calendar to introduce the *Liturgy of the Hours* in the context of praying for the dead. The feast of All Souls, Advent, and Lent are optimal times.
4. The music ministry is essential for proclaiming the Psalms in song.

Pastoral Action

Falling in love with the Psalms is really necessary for meaning in a ministry to the bereaved. Not only do they assist us in our empathic responses but also bring healing to those who are grief-stricken. When we lose someone we love, very often we feel shattered "like a vase," to use the imagery of the Psalms. The Psalms unlock our feelings and help us to express them. At the same time they help us to rebuild our trust in God. Our converse with God is given very real human cries and does not deny when we pray the Psalms. They are poetic hymns given to us that are timeless. Every age has to embrace the Psalms to be hopeful and trusting in God. We can rightly call them "voices of trust." This chapter gives us another important liturgical dimension of the Psalms.

Chapter Nine

Prayers for Special Circumstances

There are times that are more pastorally challenging than other times. At a person's death, the circumstances do make a difference. The ritual is pastorally sensitive to this reality and provides us with special prayers.

When death occurs in ways that we do not expect or contrary to our expectations, complications often happen. In the ritual, there is sensitivity to special circumstances surrounding the death (*OCF. par. 398*). The ritual lists specific incidences that are exceptionally difficult. Prayers are adapted to help the bereaved cope in ways that express the reality of loss for the mourners (*OCF. par. 399*). This chapter will highlight some of the most crucial and pastorally challenging losses. Attention will be given to the ritual's prayers and corresponding pastoral care for these circumstances.

When Suicide Occurs

The ritual specifically mentions those who die from suicide. This is an important inclusion. Many people still think that Christian burial is refused to those who die from suicide. The phrasing of the previous sentence illustrates how thinking has evolved. Notice that death is "from" suicide. No longer do we refer to someone as having "committed" suicide. The presumption is in favor of the person not deliberately taking his/her life. Illness and the limitations of the human condition are considered. God's love overcomes all estrangement.

The prayers are comforting those who feel the sadness and violence of such a death. The mourners are included in the prayer (O.C.F. par.398 #44-45). The image of God as the lover of souls is a source of consolation amidst an otherwise totally chaotic event.

When someone we love chooses to take their own life, reactions from survivors can be more complicated. Survivors have to deal with aspects that are beyond the usual grief process. There is the social stigma, anger towards the deceased or themselves, and guilt at not having prevented it. The mourners have a lot that has to be discussed. Meeting with the survivors requires helping them release feelings and authentically make them their own.

The pastoral caregiver is present to help the bereaved. It is not a time to be judgmental. Most caregivers are kind and empathic. They can, however, inadvertently slip into a judgmental mode and not even be aware that they are doing so. A subtle and harmful way to be judgmental is to say: "Mary must have been very ill to do this," or "John was so overwhelmed in his mental illness that he really did not know what he was doing."

While the above may well be true, it is not helpful to console in that way. Survivors very often have fear for their own mental health. When we console by making judgments, fear and anxiety are often heightened. It is necessary to be aware of this before we meet with surviving families. Prayer and placing the loss Into God's hands is far more comforting. The prayer in the ritual is carefully constructed and very suitable as prayer that consoles.

It goes without saying that all deaths from suicide are not the same. Sometimes there is a history of attempts. Others are due to severe physical illness, while some suicides are cries for help resulting in death. Those who survive want to know the circumstances. This is in accordance with normal searching and wondering about death during bereavement. Survivors wonder for a variety of reasons, among them inheritability and guilt.

There are some important ideas for the pastoral caregiver to recall when intervening with family survivors:

1. Remember that the survivors are probably shocked. Suicide is a sudden death.
2. The survivors need to sort out their feelings. Give them time to adjust to what is happening.
3. Help survivors not to make quick decisions. This depends upon the timeframe. If you meet with them at the hospital or home, they may not be clear about what funeral arrangements to make.
4. Encourage a public funeral. They will receive support and consolation from friends and relatives. The rituals will initiate the grieving process. Also, the bereaved need to realize that Christian burial is not denied a person who dies in this way.
5. Offer ongoing support through follow-up pastoral visits.
6. Support groups for survivors assist them in doing the necessary grief work.

When Death Occurs After a Long Illness

These prayers (*OCF*, par.398; 39-41) are particularly appropriate for many serious illnesses. Along with cancer, heart disease, strokes, and other illnesses, we ought to consider AIDS for these prayers. The prayers give insight to the long suffering that people go through while dying. It is necessary to admit and accept the losses and transformation of all pain and suffering. Such images are healing and hopeful for the mourners as they recall the illness.

Certain prolonged illnesses, for a variety of reasons (AIDS and otherwise) cause family division. The deceased, in many instances, was committed to AIDS education. After the death, some family members feel uneasy and either withdraw or argue with others about publicity being heaped on the family. In these instances, anger as an expression of grief can affect family members, possibly in a permanent way.

There are some very real misconceptions about funeral arrangements for AIDS victims. I had occasion to speak with an AIDS support group, and I thought I was there to communicate ways of healing and coping with loss. Instead, the most significant question was regarding church burial. The group was composed of men who wondered if the Catholic Church would allow them to be buried with Church rituals, since they were homosexual in their lifestyle. This meeting took place in the 1980s. Since then, the fact of so many Christian burials for all those victims of AIDS ought to provide people with the answer. Yet there are family members and victims who wonder how the funeral can be conducted.

The pastoral caregiver's best of all possible scenarios is to meet with parish groups and prearrange funerals. Those families who are suffering with a loved one's prolonged death sometimes welcome being better prepared. This is a difficult and sensitive pastoral practice. The best way to help these families is to offer prearranging or liturgy preparation evenings for funerals during Lent. It is a healthy way for mourners to get some much needed anticipatory grief work.[45]

It is important, after prolonged suffering, to say goodbye. The funeral farewell is the time for family members to do this. It is suggested that family members type up a few pages; reading is usually less stressful. The farewell ought to mirror how the deceased accepted his/her Christian faith. I recall one liturgy where I mentioned anointing an AIDS victim who, even though there was an IV in his arm raised it to bless himself. His family and friends knew this was a testimony of faith towards the end of his earthly journey.

The farewell is not meant to be a eulogy. That is not to say that we exclude mentioning personal characteristics and creative gifts possessed by the deceased. The farewell done during the final commendation is a healing moment for families and friends. It releases the emotions and emptiness that accompany lengthy illness.

A Sudden Death: Age Related Deaths

The ritual offers prayers for people who die at different times in the lifespan. Someone may be young (*OCF*, par.398, #27-28) or, as we noted, an infant, stillbirth, or miscarriage. When we include the circumstance such as age, it personalizes the ritual for the deceased's memory and the mourners recollections.

---

[45] Walter Smith, *AIDS Living & Dying With Hope*, Paulist Press, New York, New Jersey1988 p.72

When young people die, more support ought to be offered. At young ages when they are on the threshold of adulthood, peer relationships are often the most important. They are in the process of becoming more outer directed toward their relationships away from family connections.

I recall an automobile accident when two teenage boys were killed. The principal of the high school offered help, and the guidance counselors and local clergy worked together with the deceased's friends and classmates.

Young people usually respond in remarkable ways when there is a funeral. They take part and console families. If the teenager participated in sports programs or other activities, mention is noted. The Farewell and Final Commendation or the Committal allows the bereaved friends to say goodbye.

Farewell Reflections

Lately the actual time to offer a reflection has been debated. There are opinions that the reflection ought to take place before the funeral mass when everyone is seated. In this way it be separated from the liturgy which is devoted to praying for the deceased not eulogizing them. Others think that time may be given at the vigil. Still other opinions are that the farewell reflection is best served in the cemetery or at the reception following the committal service.

There are many reasons as to why this is being addressed. Unfortunate inappropriate remarks have been made. It also within the liturgy has been done incorrectly with a number of people wanting to speak. Along with that has been the time factor. Some remarks have been far too long. Perhaps the most difficult part of this is the fact that guidelines are needed as to how to compose a liturgical and faith type of reflection. In my work entitled *Planning the Catholic Funeral* there is a section dedicated to just that concern.

Ongoing support for young deaths is accomplished in a variety of ways. Living memorials through scholarships and other awards are ways to remember the young person.

Death of a Spouse

The prayers for the death of a spouse (*OCF*, 398, #34-35) reflect the prayers at the time of marriage. Recently I attended a funeral of a woman who had just celebrated her fiftieth wedding anniversary.

Pictures of the celebration were posted for those visiting the funeral home. Such a recollection illustrated the happiness in remembering that occasion. It helps the mourners remember more vividly the deceased whom they loved in life.

When someone we love dies, it is very important to make the funeral as personal as possible. Photographs, poetry, favorite hymns, and other gestures ought to be included. This is very much in keeping with the psychology of loss. Sometimes our remembrance of the loved one is very keen early on in our grief. It has been noted that the loss makes the loved one even more present than ever. We recall things we thought were long forgotten, such as mannerisms, gestures, and even remarks. This is a very intense and significant part of the grieving process. Our liturgical worship is of great assistance for the bereaved, especially in allowing them ways to express their grief.

The death of a spouse requires continual support. Age is a factor in making adjustments. There are some excellent support groups, such as Parents Without Partners. Parishes and agencies also have Widow to Widow Programs and other grief caring groups.

Widows and widowers intensely feel the effects of being alone. Physical health and depression may be noticed. They need more than family involvement. The parish is often the vehicle for their being able to mange their losses.

Relationships

Various members of the community, according to their relationships, are noted. Religious leaders such as the pope, bishops, priests, and deacons are prayed for according to their vocations. The vocations to married life and parenthood are noted in a special way.

The list of special prayers also includes sudden and violent deaths. What the ritual is doing is taking into considerations circumstances and helping the bereaved to once again place the losses into the broader context of religious faith.

Pastoral Action

This chapter has explored some of the losses we experience, either personally or in our families. The special circumstances highlight the intensity of suffering that members of the community experience in the uniqueness of their loss. Real consolation occurs when we realize such losses and pray with the bereaved. These prayers assist the entire community in being more connected and conscious of loss for others. They have a sensitivity to the type of loss the bereaved are going through. This makes the funeral more personal. There is a uniqueness to every funeral and they need to be personalized for those who are mourning. This chapter needs to be referred to when we are planning a funeral for a family.

Chapter Ten

Grief Ministry in the Parish

This chapter provides the reader with an overview as to the many ways a viable grief ministry program can serve the spiritual needs of the parish. It assists caregivers with a variety of choices as to where to minister. It is a chapter to aid those who want to minister to find their place in the ministry of consolation.

In every parish there are a number of service groups. The Eucharistic ministers visit and bring communion to the sick. These elderly and homebound persons experience many losses. The Eucharistic minister is the person who can be supportive to the bereaved through ongoing visits.

It is necessary for those who minister to express their grief at the loss of a parishioner with whom there existed a ministry bond. One clear example of this type of grieving was expressed in our parish.

Helen, the Eucharistic minister, visited Sadie every week for two and a half years She did this faithfully every Sunday after the parish liturgy. When Sadie died, Helen was heartbroken with the loss of this relationship. The pastor invited Helen to be the Eucharistic minister at Sadie's funeral. This was very helpful for Helen, who interpreted her presence as a farewell to Sadie as she went forth to the Kingdom.

Models of care ought to be integrated into the rituals for the parish community. The community's presence at funeral liturgies connects the bereaved to the parish community. The parish is really gathering together when the community responds to the needs of the bereaved. The concern for the bereaved is an overall characteristic of the *Order of Christian Funerals*. Throughout the ritual, mention is given to those left behind. Prayers are offered and meaning given to families and friends. The ritual possesses a vision of caring and connecting all who are involved in the mystery of death and resurrection. The ritual is in itself pastoral care, which continues into the ongoing community ministry. One pastor very clearly noted this when the ritual was promulgated.

> Promulgation is a simple matter of church law, a date that is set to being using the new text, usually accompanied by an official decree forbidding the continued use of the previous ritual. But the reception of a liturgical text is more the work of the Spirit than of ecclesiastical decree makers. Reception usually takes years and even generations, as the vision and spirit of a new liturgical rite is gradually assimilated into the fabric of Christian life and experience.Promulgation of the Order of Christian Funerals now offers parishes the opportunity to begin work on the task of reception.[46]

Support and healing occur when the parish journeys with the bereaved from the critical time of loss to after the funeral, when pastoral visitors contact families. The companionship or

---

46 Marilyn Kofler, Kevin O'Connor, *Handbook for Ministers of Care*, Chicago, Liturgy Training Publications, 1987, p. 9

covenant for caring for the bereaved is envisioned by the ritual. This requires pastoral planning and structures that help the bereaved reorganize their lives.

Bereavement Committee

Every parish is greatly assisted by having a Bereavement Committee to coordinate the ministries for the bereaved. The committee reflects the community's intention to offer support for those suffering during a critical period.

This committee may be a separate standing group or a subcommittee of the Parish Pastoral Council. The membership provides the necessary pastoral leadership, ensuring that care is given.

The ministry of consolation includes the entire parish community. It is a ministry for the entire parish to become involved with. The mistaken idea that clergy or pastoral staff are the exclusive ministers defeats the real meaning of this ministry. There are many good candidates for membership on the committee. Parish Council members, physicians, professional counselors, social workers, and nurses are good candidates for membership.

It ought to be clear from the start that membership means working in partnership with the community. The team approach illustrates that we are called two by two to go preach the Gospel of healing and consolation. The committee will assist in coordinating the following parish ministries with the pastoral staff. This is a collaborative ministry, which means being willing to share resources and ideas in a creative way.

Parish Grief Management Ministries

Parish programs may simply be called a "Lazarus Group" or another suitable name. These parishioners would cook a meal and drop it off at the bereaved house.

Or the group may set up the parish hall for the gathering after the funeral. This could entail simply putting out the coffee and arranging the settings for possibly caterers or friends of the family. Other services may include hour sitting during a funeral or picking someone up at the airport.

Pastoral Visitors

More involved ministries, such as a pastoral visit, require that workshops or days of recollection be scheduled. The Bereavement Committee may collaborate with other committees on the Parish Pastoral Council.

Consequently, a day of recollection developed by a Spiritual Life Committee may develop themes connected to separation and loss. Speakers may be scheduled to help the parish understand the nature of grief. The more familiar parishioners are with the process, the better equipped they are to be effective pastoral visitors.

The pastoral visitor is a key person for parish grief ministry. It is he or she who journeys with the bereaved from the beginning to the time of readjustment to the loss. It takes time to do this. Being a pastoral visitor to the bereaved requires developing some very specific skills, along with considerable empathy. Training and support from the parish is a very definite necessity.

Spiritual Ongoing Formation Program

The correct impression ought to be conveyed to those who want to be trained as pastoral visitors. The pastoral visit or consolation call is ministry. Pastoral psychology plays a significant role, too. The primary emphasis, however, remains spiritual. Consequently, in developing a training (formation program) it is very important to let spirituality manifested by compassion and love take precedence. Some ideas to keep in mind are the following:

---

1. *Contact parishioners whom you feel would be willing to be pastoral visitors.*
2. *Arrange a parish meeting for discussing the role of the pastoral visitor in the ministry of consolation.*
3. *Explain the phases of grief ministry in the parish. Communicate how support to do the ministry will be provided by seminar type discussion sessions.*

The following format may be followed:

Meeting One: The initial meeting may take place at a parish day of recollection. The day may consist of morning and afternoon sessions concluding with liturgy. The intent will be to develop a spirituality rooted in scripture. Along with this spirituality, emphasis maybe given to the pastoral psychology of bereavement. This entails communicating about crisis ministry

Meeting Two: The phases of the ministry of consolation may be explored at these meetings:

Critical Phase: How to relate to the bereaved when you first meet with them at the time of death. Some crisis intervention skills of being attentive to the bereaved may be explored. Helping the bereaved become oriented to the loss is very important at this time.

Liturgical: This phase includes liturgical preparation. The pastoral visitor/caregiver may provide options from the *Order of Christian Funerals*. Familiarity with the ritual moments and parish role in accompanying the deceased Christian, along with family and friends, is a necessity. There is a need to have the ritual and minister together in planning the Catholic funeral.

Meeting Three: The pastoral visit or the "condolence call" is very important for the ministry of consolation. This session is an opportune time for some role playing. Important questions ought to be faced regarding how to approach the bereaved. Should they be left alone? What is the purpose of the pastoral visit? Do we give permission to grieve? How can we be a compassionate listener?

Meeting Four: This meeting will continue to explore ways of communicating with the bereaved. It will help the pastoral visitor to develop a healing ministry. This can be done by cultivating some communication skills. Role playing will be helpful in acquiring good listening skills. Three aspects of (1) paying attention to the other person by physically using body language and eye contact, (2) notifying the other that you have heard them through gestures such as nodding or other body language, and (3) developing a rapport by asking questions and allowing reflection will be explored.

Some Overall Guidelines for a Bereavement Visit

1. Always call first and offer to set up a time to visit. Identify yourself as a representative of the parish.
2. Be empathic in your visit. Try to imagine what it is like for the bereaved person at this time.
3. Bring along some information you can leave behind (Care Notes, Christopher Notes, Catholic Updates, or a prayer booklet, such as *A Way of the Cross for the Bereaved*).
4. Notice how the bereaved is adjusting. Be familiar with symptoms and observations regarding grief.
5. Allow the bereaved to talk about the loss.
6. Inquire how they are doing since the funeral. This opens up conversation about doing the tasks associated with grief work. Acceptance may be evident if they are getting affairs in order with social security, pension, the deceased's personal effects, etc. This may be accomplished without prying into the bereaved person's life, instead recognizing these topics when they occur as aspects of good grief work. The bereaved may need your assistance in many matters, even in sending out thank you notes to those who consoled during the funeral.
7. Above all, be yourself. This means developing self confidence and not trying to role play or be overly solicitous. Ministry means being a compassionate listener.

8. Offer to pray with the bereaved. You may want to pick an appropriate Psalm. Psalm Twenty Three would be prayed for guidance. If there are still real difficulties in acceptance, you may choose Psalm 130, "Out of the Depths," or Psalm 22. The Psalms open up a special spirituality for the bereaved, which helps them in expressing their feelings to God. The Psalms relate to feelings of anger, abandonment, and rebuilding trust.
9. Suggest that the bereaved consider becoming a member of the Parish Support Group (Caring Group) for the bereaved. Remember: it is an offer, not a command. They may or may not be ready to accept the invitation. Offer to return again and visit with them.

The Parish Support Group Ministry

The parish support group exemplifies what it means to be a caring, supportive community. The bereaved members start out as individuals who have loss in common. As time goes by, they become a group of people bonded together by compassion and love. Healing occurs as they reach out and express through tear-filled eyes the experiences of loneliness, abandonment, anger, guilt, and yearning to be with a deceased loved one. The group becomes a microcosm of what we hope the parish will become.

Establishing a support group can be done in very uncomplicated ways. If we follow through with some pastoral planning, the parish can be functioning with a group almost before we know it. We should allow at least two months ahead of our proposed starting date. The facilitators, who ideally have a background in social work or counseling, have to make certain time commitments. They ought to meet every other week to develop topics for the group and discuss ways of facilitating. Some topics may include:

Possible Support Group Topics

- *Grief and the way I respond*
- *Remembering and Letting Go*
- *Holidays, Holy Days, and Their Effects*
- *Channeling Anger, Guilt, and Abandonment Emotions*
- *Crying Out to God*
- *After Loss: Living and Loving Again*

These topics ought to receive publicity in the parish bulletin and local media. It is essential that the consciousness of the community be elevated to an awareness of the needs of the bereaved. Everyone ought to be aware that such a service is offered. Caring groups are usually scheduled for six sessions. It is best to have the sessions occur over a ten- to twelve-week period. Meeting every other week helps the participants not to be too intense in doing grief work.[47]

When sessions are not occurring, participants can contact other members for support. Sometimes a telephone call or a cup of coffee together is very healing. It brings about a closeness and breaks down the barriers of being isolated while grieving.

Establishing a caring group promotes ways to mutually support others in the parish who are undergoing similar losses. It provides needed insights into the grieving process to heighten

---

[47] Terence Curley. "Establishing a Caring Group to Support the Bereaved," *Pastoral Life*, Vol. 40, No.10, Nov. 1991, p.17

transitions. It gives a spiritual dimension to the grief work to spark spiritual growth during a difficult time of life. The importance of receiving spiritual guidance within a group cannot be overstated. The group is led primarily by the Holy Spirit, who is the Comforter.

Accepting the Ritual

We noted in the beginning of this chapter how there is considerable difference between accepting and promulgating a change in the Church. The ritual's vision is encouraging for the role of the community. New ministries and new pastoral care ought to occur due to the ritual. That is not to say that everything that ought to be done by the ritual has happened. No one ritual can be complete. It is better to take a dynamic approach and consider the ritual as a process. The more we ritualize, the more the Holy Spirit will guide us toward amplifying what has been developed. This is clearly evident when we see the need to ritualize deaths due to miscarriages and stillbirths.

When a caregiver takes a "Lone Ranger" approach to the ministry, this ritual cannot be effectively implemented. The ritual is meant to be the community's ministry. The initial meetings with the bereaved, stations for prayers, follow-up visits, and support groups are all the workings of the baptized, not necessarily ordained members of the parish community. Inroads for our understanding of ministry with the lay ecclesial ministers have greatly changed our appreciation of the depth and width of ministry in our day. The document by the Catholic Bishops of the United States entitled *Co-Workers in the Vineyard of the Lord* is a hallmark for our implementing ministry according to the vision and intent of Vatican II. We see this especially in grief ministry, which makes explicit our journey begun in baptism. Everyone is called to help others in a dynamic manner. The more we interpret this in a dynamic way, the more understandable and effective ministry will be for us.

Pastoral Action

Pastoral care is the work of the entire community. If we are to follow the guidance of the ritual, we will need to do so as a community. It is meant for the community to reach out and care for those who are grieving. This chapter illustrates the real meaning of participation and ministry as hallmarks for the ritual and ongoing pastoral care. The importance of the lay ecclesial ministry cannot be emphasized enough as an expression of the real meaning of the People of God theology given to us by the Second Vatican Council. Our hope is with the kind and compassionate ministry which is at the heart of the parish.

Chapter Eleven

Cremation and Bodily Resurrection

This chapter addresses the theology of resurrection of the body in accordance with our Christian beliefs. It is a very important passage for pastoral care for the bereaved. This chapter highlights the ritual and belief aspects so necessary for the bereaved at a critical time in their lives.

Since the promulgation of the *Order of Christian Funerals* (1989) and the issuance of guidelines for cremation (1997), considerably new interest in the practice of this burial is occurring.

It has been clear for many years that cremation was a practice condemned and forbidden by the Church. With its allowance now, people are asking why this reversal is permitted. What has changed? Many of us vaguely remember how cremation was taught as forbidden by the Church since the practice in the mind of pagans denied that there would be a resurrection on the last day. While it was confusing, especially when we knew that the bodies of our ancestors had already turned to dust, we nevertheless accepted the prohibition.

Throughout history, cremation did play a part in influencing faith and belief among Christians. For many centuries cremation was a clear statement that the bodily resurrection did not occur. That historical statement has dimmed in meaning in recent times, enough so that the Church is now willing to accept the practice. A brief historical review will offer us some explanation and perspective.

Looking back to the early days of the Church, we realize there were two prevailing reasons for the Church not to accept this practice. The first was the fact that the Church was a very small minority within a large pagan culture. That culture for the most part did not hold to beliefs in the afterlife; as such, cremation was an appropriate burial method.

In contrast, early Church members saw their identity intimately connected to an afterlife and resurrection of the body. With such an identity, burial was the only option. This option was further chosen as the more normal one for the early Church, since most of its members were Semitic and burial was the prevailing norm for this group of people.

What we then had was the natural inclination to stay with an accepted practice that also strongly contradicted the pagan practice of the day. This contrast was further heightened when martyrs' bodies were cremated as a further humiliation to Christians. The catacombs, as a sacred place of burial, bear witness to the importance of and reverence early Christians had for the body in death.

Around the fifth century, following the earlier conversion of Constantine, the practice of cremation ceased in the Roman Empire. In 789, Charlemagne made it a capital offense to follow pagan rituals for cremating a body.

For the next thousand years, cremation was abandoned as a practice in Europe. There is some evidence of the Church reaffirming the condemnation during the pontificate of Boniface VIII (c.1300).

Recent Changes

Proponents of cremation were still seen as proposing something that was not compatible with Christian burial. The 1917 Code of Canon Law (Canon 1203) condemned cremation. Since that time, there was little discussion of cremation until recent developments.

In 1963, during the Second Vatican Council, the prohibition against cremation was lifted, provided that the choice to cremate was not done in contradiction to Christian belief. To meet this provision, a person, when preparing for his or her own death and burial, would usually write a statement attesting that the cremation requested did not deny the resurrection but was made for other reasons. As long as the cremation did not constitute a denial of the resurrection, permission was usually granted.

This, however, was not a widespread practice, since the Church still recommended that the body be buried. As a sign of its continuing displeasure in this practice, no prayers were designated for cremated remains (cremains). All prayers were offered prior to the cremation of the body.

In 1969, there were further changes concerning cremation. The *Ordo Exsequiarum* added prayers to the be offered at the cremation and at the time of burial (committal prayers), though still the Church did not encourage cremation as norm for burial. The latest revision of the *Order of Christian Funerals* (1989) still upholds the traditional way of burial, yet it does so with considerable leeway for the process of cremation.

New Considerations

Now the spotlight has once again been thrown on the practice of cremation. In examining current beliefs and practices, the Church no longer sees the practice as an espousal of pagan abominations. We as a community of believers have moved forward. And while holding to the traditional beliefs, we are in the process of "traditioning" forward.

In this process, the Church stays young and vital by always examining scripture and history as it seeks to unlock traditional beliefs for a new generation of believers. In unlocking those beliefs for this age, we go forward, ever mindful of Jesus' words spoken through scripture and tradition throughout the ages.

While pagan practices have diminished and no longer color the meaning of cremation, it still remains vitally important that we have an understanding of our belief in the bodily resurrection, no matter what our choice is. With this in mind, let us examine the biblical perspective.

Having a Biblical View of the Body

While we explore the New Testament meaning of the resurrection of the body, we must keep in mind current concerns among believers. Are cremation and bodily resurrection compatible? How can we proclaim our identity as a Church founded on resurrectional faith around this practice?

The biblical view of the body goes beyond philosophical speculation. Western philosophy tends to categorize the human person with speculation about body, mind, and spirit. On the other hand, biblical anthropology always asserts that there is basic unity between the body and soul. For the Hebrew mind, the soul is never seen as imprisoned in the body. In the Greek outlook, the soul is a prisoner and needs to be freed.

The scriptures always assert that the body is good and a part of God's creation. According to this view, it is inconceivable to think about the body as annihilated at death. There is a wholeness to the human body that continues.

The Scriptures go beyond our thinking of the body as merely fleshy substance. In our bodies, we communicate with the living God. This communication does not cease when biological death occurs.

When we hold to a "biblical perspective," we cannot entertain thoughts of our bodies being annihilated even after death. The practice of cremation really is not a challenge to our belief in the continuation of the whole person. Keeping this perspective in mind, cremation is just something that happens to the husk when the true person is gone.

Manner of Resurrection

How we view the continuation of life and the belief in the resurrection of the body is a significant topic for contemporary belief, both within the Church and in our secular society. These beliefs say much more about how we view ourselves and where we stand in our appreciation of the afterlife.

Living according to the flesh or according to the spirit is a major theme in Paul's writings. It is more than applicable to our appreciation of bodily resurrection. Resurrection is placed into its proper context, especially in Paul's First Letter to the

Corinthians. The following words are very relevant to those who wonder about the corporeal aspects of our being:

> But someone may say, "How are the dead raised? With what kind of body will they come back?" You fool! What you sow is not brought to life unless it dies. And what you sow is not the body that is to be but a bare kernel of wheat, perhaps, or some other kind; but God gives it a body as he chooses, and to each of the seeds its own body (1 Cor.15:3-38).

Father Raymond Brown, in his work *The Virginal Conception and the Bodily Resurrection of Jesus*, cites Pope Paul VI's remarks on the difficulties we have in conceptualizing resurrection:

> Jesus rose again in the same body He had from the same body He had from the Blessed Virgin, but in new conditions, vivified by a new and immortal animation, which imposes on Christ's flesh the laws and energies of the Spirit. This new reality is so far above our capacities of knowledge and even imagination that it is necessary to make room for it in our minds through faith.[48]

Theological Reflection

It is always an important theological task for every age to develop the Church's theology of death. We believe that the Lord Jesus "will change our mortal bodies to like his in glory" (cf. *Order of Christian Funerals,* no.218A) The ritual gives us certain insights that the believing community can appreciate

---

[48] Raymond Brown, *The Virginal Conception and the Bodily Resurrection*, Paulist Press, N.J., 1972

in faith. The formulation of our beliefs will grow as the Spirit directs us with new ways to express ourselves.

The allowance of cremation challenges us to evangelize within and outside of the community of faith about bodily resurrection. As we reflect both theologically and pastorally on the practice of cremation, we are faced with the task of walking a fine line: the body in death is cherished and yet cremation, while an option, does not deny the resurrection of the death.

Encountering the Glorified Lord

New Testament accounts describe the transformation of Jesus' body. After the Resurrection, when Jesus appeared to Mary Magdalene, He instructs her not to cling to Him. He was going to the Father (see Jn.20:17).

The appearance to the apostles in the locked room also describes transformative aspects. Even though there was no way to enter the room, Jesus stands in their midst. The bodily resurrection is firmly asserted with Thomas and his examining of Jesus' hands and the wound in His side.

These accounts, along with other references, illustrate the belief in the bodily resurrection. It is this resurrection faith around which the whole Church was formed. More than the empty tomb is the encounter with the glorified Lord, which inculcated our lasting belief that our bodies, even in death, will be transformed into glory.

Cremation and the Pastoral Dimension

The U.S. Bishop's Committee on Liturgy published a pamphlet entitled *Reflections on the Body, Cremation, and Catholic*

Funeral Rite This helpful resource notes that in general cremation is used (at that time) in 20 percent of all funerals in the United States. Every year that percentage increases. There are a variety of reasons for this dramatic increase.

Informal surveys show people choosing cremation not so much to avoid bodily corruption in the grave but for economic reasons. The high cost of funerals is driving some to consider cremation from a purely financial viewpoint. Cremation can reduce the cost of burial. When this occurs as it does more and more, especially among the poor, then there is the further pastoral challenge of some survivors feeling guilty about such a choice. Modern society, with its focus on goods and services, is rapidly making a traditional funeral and burial into a luxury many will not be able to afford.

Cremation is an option, and sometimes a necessity if determined by finances. Our challenge is to ensure that it does not become an end in itself. Our "disposable" society probably would not mind if funerals became a purely secular event, where the body could be simply disposed of without ritual.

Cremation is an option according to the most recent addition to the *Order of Christian Funerals.* The sacred sense of burial, as well as bodily resurrection is what the Church wants to uphold. For this reason certain guidelines are given.

It is recommended that the body be cremated after the funeral liturgies are celebrated. This is a way of affirming our belief that the body in death should be respected as an image of God. Before burial, we reverently bring the body to the sacred setting of the church. It should also be noted that viewing the body usually is of considerable help to the bereaved.

Even though the body being present is preferred, there are other options. Provisions are now made for the liturgy to be offered in the presence of the cremated remains.

> Although cremation is now permitted by the Church, it does not enjoy the same value as the burial of the body. The Church clearly prefers and urges that the body of the deceased be present for funeral rites, since the presence of the human body better expresses the values which the Church affirms in those rites.
>
> (Appendix for the *Order of Christian Funerals*, no. 413).

Now looked upon in a different way in our time, cremation can teach many how to better appreciate resurrection. Rather than seeing cremation as merely an acceptable practice, we can use it as a catalyst for reflection.

As Catholics, we need to reflect on our stated belief in the Apostle's Creed, in the resurrection of the body. Resurrection is the glorification of our earthly body, God's glorifying is absolute, and all things are possible with God.

We are always, and in every generation, growing in faith. Faith seeking understanding about bodily resurrection can only be enhanced as we reflect about bodily resurrection in the context of eternal glorification.[49]

---

[49] Terence Curley, "Cremation and Bodily Resurrection," *The Priest*, Vol.55, No.4, April 1999, p. 34

Pastoral Action

Whenever I offer a funeral liturgy for a person whose body had been cremated, I find it to be a moment of catechesis. Our parishes still have people who need to see that this practice is allowed. They also need to have some faith understanding about the mystery of the resurrection. We share in a similar resurrection to our risen Lord. Consequently, it is meaningful to mention that Jesus was raised up and appeared in glorified form. We, too, need to look forward to when our earthly bodies will be glorified. This chapter presents a framework for living within the mystery.

Chapter Twelve

St. Paul and the Ministry of Consolation

This chapter focuses on St. Paul and his ongoing contribution for ways effectively participate in the ministry of consolation. St. Paul provides us with ways to rebuild our lives in hope-filled ways with a healing spirituality for a peace beyond understanding.

The year of 2009 had been designated by Pope Benedict XVI as a jubilee for St. Paul. It marked the celebration of the Apostle to the Gentiles bi-millennium of his birth. The pontiff had instructed the faithful to imitate the apostolic zeal of this great saint. At the same time, we were to recall during this year special descriptions of St. Paul's lasting and ever relevant contribution to the Church. The Holy Father had asked us during this year to especially imitate the zeal that characterized St. Paul's life and ministry.

In this chapter, the focus is on a very significant area that shouldn't be overlooked Paul, in his life and writings, is an appropriate saint for us to conclude this book with. In St. Paul there is a timeless quality that translates into speaking to all time about loss and a deep spirituality for life's many difficulties.

St. Paul's theology offers us an underpinning for the way we minister to those suffering from life's separations and losses. His words, as is evident in his letters, illustrate the deep pastoral sensitivity he possessed for those who are shattered due to the loss of a loved one. St. Paul provides us with spirituality for reaching out to those experiencing loss.

The ministry of consolation relies on St. Paul's words to provide guidance in caring for the bereaved. Parishes will find a rich resource in faith when they explore and meditate on the Pauline letters.

Paul and a Life of Loss

Paul and those who were his disciples emphasized the importance of sanctifying life in this world in preparation for the eternal life of glory. It is with St. Paul that we are familiar with putting everything into perspective when we live with his words: "Now we see indistinctly, as in a mirror; then we shall see face to face. My knowledge is imperfect now; then I shall know even as I am known" (I Cor. 13.12-13). The words of this saint and martyr comfort us when we realize he shared our feelings of only being able to glimpse the bright promise we will someday see face to face. He acknowledges our loss and inability to fully understand what we are experiencing. He has been there, knows the feeling, but his faith sustains and pulls him forward. We, too, can make it through this darkness.

In his physical and spiritual intensity for evangelizing, St. Paul knew about loss. Loss was a major part of Paul's life and ministry. He recounts many of his losses in (II Corinthians 11:23-29) and how much he endured. He writes of being beaten with rods, shipwrecked three times, hit by stones, and living with hunger, cold, and hardship on an almost constant basis.

The Pauline missionary effort shows us a model of how to detach and surrender to the will of God. Our attachments cannot be allowed to obscure our relationship with God. St. Paul lived the spiritual and physical poverty, which increased his love of Christ Jesus. By having nothing, Paul gained everything. It is little wonder that Paul wrote: "I count everything as loss because of the surpassing worth of knowing Christ Jesus my Lord" (Phil3:8).

Consoling Others

In the Second Letter to the Corinthians, the origins of all consolation are spelled out to this early community of faith:

Praise be to the God and Father of our Lord Jesus Christ, the All merciful Father, the God whose consolation never fails us! He comforts us in our troubles, so that we in turn may be able to comfort others in any trouble of theirs and to share with them the consolation we ourselves received from God. As Christ's cup of suffering overflows, and we suffer with him, so also through Christ our consolation overflows.

(II Cor. 1; 3-6).

By embracing Christ's suffering as our own and offering our suffering to Christ, we free ourselves to accept Christ's love and consolation, which is without limit. The grace we receive transforms our suffering into acceptance and brings us closer to seeing clearly our union with our loved ones in Christ.

Pastoral Dimension

As priests, we are more than familiar with the readings from St. Paul in the lectionary for funeral masses. St. Paul's words are pastorally very significant and put into focus our basic beliefs as Christians in the resurrection. Very often the community gathered for funerals is in great need of catechesis. As God's holy people, we want to evangelize those who are present as to how we believe and how those beliefs guide our earthly journeys. We can attribute to St. Paul the wonderfully poignant question (Paul to the Romans 6:3-4, 8-9), "Are you unaware that we who were baptized into Christ Jesus were baptized into his death?" He continues, "We were indeed buried with him through baptism into his death, so that, just as Christ was raised from the dead by the glory of the Father, we too might live in newness of life."

Paul raises the consciousness of the community with his question. It also catechizes as to the signs and symbols for our *Order of Christian Funerals.* The selfsame symbols used at the beginning of our faith journey are now being utilized in the funeral liturgy. We are now recalling throughout the liturgy our participation in the Paschal Mystery. The white garment worn at baptism, now symbolized in the pall, the holy water, and the paschal candle, is a sacred reminder that we were incorporated into the Body of Christ through baptism. Paul reminds us that death has been with us from the beginning. It is our passage. It is our destiny. At the same time we are raised and able to live eternally in Christ. We live our lives with death before us but we also live with eternity in our sights as well. We are graced creatures who see through faith-filled eyes.

In the funeral vigil, we can read from Paul's second letter to the Corinthians: "So we are always courageous, although we know that while we are at home in the body we are away from the Lord, for we walk by faith not by sight." (II Cor.5, 6-10, *Order of Christian Funerals,* par. 74).

Our homilies and liturgical catechesis is very dependant upon St. Paul and how he instructed his communities of faith in his ministry and letters. It is really remarkable how needed this message continues to be and how St. Paul framed everything so well for our present ministry to the bereaved.

Ministry and Participation

In the general introduction to the *Order of Christian Funerals* (*OCF*, par.,1-8) the ritual highlights the suffering of the bereaved and the community response. The importance of caring for one another is evident when St. Paul's words from 1Corinthians 12:26 are noted:"If one member suffers in the Body of Christ which is the Church, all the members suffer with that member." This is the pastoral perspective for the ministry summarized very empathically by St. Paul. These words serve us well when we initiate and deepen ministries of care programs for our parishioners who are suffering loss. This is in keeping with St. Paul's theology, which teaches us to focus on the Cross, where there is healing and hope for those who are ministering or suffering.

The Message of Hope

St. Paul places grief into the context of hope. He does this in his letter to the Thessalonians. It was evident to Paul when he stayed in Thessalonica that some of the people who were grieving were not taking into consideration their faith in the Lord. They grieved on a worldly plane. By doing so they were not open to experiencing the love of Christ and His consolation. Paul was writing to admonish those who were grieving in this manner. He gives us the message that we proclaim as well to our communities of faith:

We would have you be clear about those who sleep in death, brothers; otherwise you might yield to grief, like those who have no hope. For if we believe that Jesus died and rose, God will bring forth with him from the dead those who have fallen asleep believing in him."

(1 Thessalonians 4:13-15).

It is the Resurrection that brings about our hope for eternal life. We are to "console one another with this message"(1 Thessalonians 4:17). St. Paul gives us words of consolation that directly instill hope for the bereaved. In our prayer with the bereaved, we need to recall what Paul gives us in his letters to the first Christians and to Christians of the twenty-first century. Not only does he put our grief into perspective, but he also addresses the deep suffering being endured by those experiencing loss. We as ministers to the bereaved need to offer this wide perspective of faith that is still a vibrant and vital message.

Peace Beyond Understanding

Pastoral care and concern for the grief-stricken is clearly evident when final prayers are offered at the place of committal. The prayer is fashioned in accordance with St. Paul's Letter to the Philippians 4.6-8

The Lord is near; have no anxiety, but in everything make your requests known to God in prayer and petition with thanksgiving. Then the peace of God, which is beyond our utmost understanding, will guard over your hearts and your thoughts, in Christ Jesus.

The actual prayer from the ritual reads: "May the peace of God which is beyond all understanding, keep your hearts and minds in the knowledge and love of God and of his Son, our Lord Jesus Christ. Amen" (*Order of Christian Funerals,* par. 326). We have noted this as the title for this book. It clearly puts our loss into the context of faith. Our continual prayer is that we will receive this blessing from God.

During difficult times for the bereaved, when all seems dark and bleak, Paul admonishes us, as he did the Thessalonians and Philippians, to keep Christ close to configure our sufferings and loss to Christ on the cross, knowing as we do that the resurrection dawns bright, making all things new.

A considerable part of grief is trying to sort things out. With intense grief there is often disorientation and confusion in how we think. If we have attachments that control our lives, it makes the grieving process all the more difficult. There is a need for a spirituality that allows us to realize that by rebuilding our trust in God, we can experience the peace that is beyond understanding. God's infusion of love in Christ Jesus is what sustains us in all that we do especially while we grieve. St. Paul puts all of this into focus by the way he ministered and taught us how to live out affliction with encouragement (II Cor.1:6).

Developing a New Relationship in Faith

What I have come to believe in my years of ministering to the bereaved is that this is a time of primary spiritual need. This need to understand and move is a spiritual task. It is a need to integrate our faith and loss on both the physical and spiritual plane. Tapping into the grace of our faith, those who mourn are able to sort and realign thoughts and feelings into a more spiritual paradigm that will work for the changed and challenging circumstances facing them. That need is to have a new relationship in faith with our loved one who has died.

This spiritual task is very much in keeping with contemporary insights to loss. We are told by many theories when we lose someone, we need to accept the loss and in the grieving process reinvest our emotions once again. We need to let go of our attachments and then in letting go, not stop there but go further and invest in our new spiritual relationship with our loved ones. We hope and pray they will be raised up in glorified form, sharing in a like resurrection to our risen Lord. So much of this theology is dependant on Pauline thought. Our belief in the Paschal Mystery and our encounter with the Lord give us certain hope. "If we believe that Jesus died and rose, so too will God, through Jesus, bring with him those who have fallen asleep" (1Thessalonians 4:14).

Paul is a saint for the bereaved in his persistence and courage to continue amidst loss, always aware of his relationship with the Lord. He attributes this not to his own efforts but to the power of God. For spiritual encouragement, the bereaved need to hear Paul's words:

> The Transcendent power comes from God, not from us. We are afflicted in every way possible, but we are not crushed; we have our doubts, but we never despair; we are persecuted, but we are never forsaken; we are struck down; but we are never annihilated (II Corinthians 4:7-8).

Spirituality for Separation and Loss

Christians who grieve do so in a spiritual context. We place our losses in life into our relationship with the Lord. Paul has given the very foundations for this context. With him, we appreciate the ministry to every community of faith. His letters to the churches give us the spiritual guidance for graced strength to face whatever happens on our journey.

St. Paul's autobiographical references serve us well for establishing and forming grief ministry. He discloses for us his own belief and what he is going through as a person. He writes:

> I am convinced that neither death, nor life, nor angels, nor principalities, nor present things, nor future things, nor powers, nor height, nor depth, nor anything else in creation will be able to separate us from the love of God in Christ Jesus our Lord (Rom. 8:38-39).

St. Paul gives us a context for living, no matter what we face. His words echo those of Jesus, who reminded us that He would be with us always to the end of time.

The more we read St. Paul, the more we will become aware of how relevant his words are for an effective ministry and especially the ministry of consolation Christ crucified provides us with the power to be able to receive comfort and consolation, and communicate this as members of the Body of Christ. This is St. Paul's gift to us for our pastoral ministry to the bereaved.[50]

---

[50] Terence Curley, "St. Paul and the Ministry of Consolation," *The Priest*, Vol. 65, No.6, June 2009, p.16

Pastoral Action

We need pastoral guides for our ministry to the bereaved. In many ways, St. Paul fulfills that for us in his life and theology. In his own life he experienced many losses. The way he wrote about what happened to him is still encouraging to us in our life's journey. He places the loss into the context of faith and trust in God. So, we pray for his guidance for us. May the Peace which is beyond understanding always be with you.

Bibliography

Abbott, Walter, and Joseph Gallagher. *The Documents of Vatican II.* New York: Guild Press, 1966

Anderson, Bernhard. *Out of the Depths, The Psalms Speak for Us Today.* Philadelphia: The Westminster Press, 1983

Boadt, Lawrence, Mary Dombeck, and H. Richard Rutherford. *The Rites of Death and Dying.* Collegeville, MN: The Liturgical Press, 1988

Bruggemann, Walter. "From Hurt to Joy, From Death to Life," *Interpretation XXVIII*, no.1 (Jan.1974): 3-20

_____. *The Message of the Psalms: A Theological Commentary,* Augsburg Publishing Co., Minneapolis, 1984

Catholic Conference of Canadian Bishops. "The Christian Funeral," *National Bulletin on Liturgy 22*, no. 119 (December 1989): 197-25

Caplan, Gerald. *An Approach to Community Mental Health.* New York: Grune & Stratton, Inc., 1961

Clinebell, Howard J. *Basic Types of Pastoral Care and Counseling, Resources for The Ministry of Healing & Growth.* Nashville: Abingdon Press, 1984

Curley, Terence P. "New Funeral Ritual Means Change for Funeral Directors," *American Funeral Director.* Vol. 114, No. 3, March (1991): 24-26

_____. "When The Community Laments," *The Priest.* Nov., Vol. 47, No. 6. (1991): 32-34

_____. "Separation and Loss," *American Funeral Director.* Vol. 114, No. 11, Nov. 1991 (36)

_____. "Psalms for Separation and Loss" *The Priest.* Nov., Vol.47, No. 11, 1991 (41)

_____. "Establishing a Caring Group to Support the Bereaved," *Pastoral Life.* Vol. 40, No. 10, Nov. 1991

_____. "Music Expressing Pastoral Care for the Bereaved," *Pastoral Life.* Vol. 41, No.1, January 1992, 21-26

Curley, Terence P. *Console One Another: A Guide for Christian Funerals,* Sheed & Ward, Kansas City, MO, 1993

_____. *The Ministry of Consolation, A Parish Guide for Comforting the Bereaved,* Alba House, New York, 1993

_____. *Healing The Broken-Hearted, Consoling the Grief-Stricken,* Alba House, New York 1995

_____. *A Way of the Cross for the Bereaved,* Alba House, New York, 1997

_____. *Six Steps for Managing Loss: A Catholic Guide Through Grief,* Alba House, New York, 1997

_____. *Healing: Questions and Answers for Those Who Mourn,* Alba House, New York, 2002

_____. *The Ministry of Consolers,* The Liturgical Press (Collegeville Ministry Series), Collegeville, MN, 2004

_____. *The Ministry of Consolers,* Claretian Publications, Quezon, Philippines, 2005

_____. *Planning The Catholic Funeral,* The Liturgical Press, Collegeville, MA, 2005

_____. *Journey To Healing: A Ministry for the Bereaved* (DVD), Alba House Communications, Canfield, OH, 1996

_____. *Through The Dark Valley* (DVD), Alba House Communications, Canfield, OH, 1998

_____. *From Darkness to Light* (CD), Alba House Communications, Canfield, OH, 1998

_____. *Arise and Walk: A Christian Grieving Guide* (DVD), Alba House Communications, Canfield, OH, 2001

_____. *Finding Your Way Through Grief* (CD), Alba House Communications, Canfield, OH, 2004

Craghan, John F. *Psalms for all Seasons,* Collegeville: The Liturgical Press, 1993

Duffy, Regis. *A Roman Catholic Theology of Pastoral Care.* Philadelphia: Fortress Press, 1983

Erikson, Erik H. *Toys and Reasons Stages in the Ritualization of Experience.* New York: W.W. Norton & Co. Inc., 1977

Gilbert, Richard B., *Finding Your Way Through Grief, Healing Prayer Services for Those Who Mourn,* Ave Maria Press, Indiana 1999

Greenberg, Ira A. *Psychodrama Theory and Therapy.* New York: Behavioral Publications, 1974

Grimes, Ronald L. *Beginnings in Ritual Studies.* Washington, D.C., University Press of America. 1982

_____. "Ritual Studies." *The Encyclopedia of Religion,* 12:422-425, ed. Mircea Eliade. New York: MacMillan,1987

Grollman, Earl A. *Living When A Loved One Has Died.* Boston: Beacon Press,1977

Hoff, Lee Ann. *People In Crisis Understanding and Helping.* Reading, Mass: Addison-Wesley Publishing Company, 1984

International Commission on English in the Liturgy. *Order Of Christian Funerals.* Washington, D.C., 1989

Jernigan, Homer. "Pastoral Care and the Crises of Life." *Community Mental Health: The Role of Church and Temple*, ed. Howard Clinebell, Nashville: Abingdon Press, 1970

Jordan, Merle. *Taking on the gods, The Task of the Pastoral Counselor.* Nashville: The Abingdon Press, 1986

Jewett, Claudia. *Helping Children Cope With Separation And Loss.* Mass: Harvard Common Press, 1982

Johnson, Sherry E. *After A Child Dies Counseling Bereaved Families.* New York: Springer Publishing Company, 1987

Kubler-Ross, Elizabeth. *On Death and Dying.* New York: MacMillan, 1969

Kushner, Harold. *When Bad Things Happen To Good People.* New York Avon Books, 1981

Lewis, C.S. *A Grief Observed.* New York: Bantam Books, 1961

Lindeman, Erich. "Symptomatology and Management of Acute Grief," *American Journal of Psychiatry.* 101 (1944): 141-148

McNiff, Shaun. *The Arts In Psychotherapy.* Springfield, IL, Charles C. Thomas Publisher, 1981

Mitchell, Kenneth R. and Herbert Anderson. *All Our Losses, All Our Griefs,* Resources For Pastoral Care. Philadelphia: The Westminster Press, 1983

Parad, Howard J. *Crisis-Intervention: Selected Readings.* New York: Family Services Association of America, 1966

Parkes, Colin Murray. *Bereavement Studies of Grief in Adult Life.* New York: International Universities Press, Inc., 1972

Poust, MaryDeTurris, *Parenting a Grieving Child,* Loyola Press, Chicago, 2002

Rando, Therese A. *Grief, Dying, And Death: Clinical Interventions For Caregivers.* Illinois: Research Press Co., 1984

Robbins, Arthur. *Expressive Therapy A Creative Arts Approach to Depth-Oriented Treatment.* New York: Human Sciences Press,1986

Rutherford, Richard. *The Death of a Christian.* New York: Pueblo Publishing, 1980

Seig, Thomas H. "Preaching at Funerals: Homily or Eulogy?" *The Priest 40*, 1984: 42-44

Smith, Walter, S.J. *Dying in the Human Life Cycle.* New York: Holt, Rinehard, and Winston, 1985

_____. *Aids Living & Dying with Hope.* New York: Paulist Press, 1988

Sofield, Loughlin, and Carol Juliano. *Collaborative Ministry Skills and Guidelines.* Notre Dame: Ave Maria Press, 1987

Sullender, R. Scott. *Grief and Growth, Pastoral Resources for Emotional and Spiritual Growth.* New York: Paulist Press, 1985

Switzer, David. *The Minister As Crisis Counselor.* Nashville: Abingdon Press, 1974

Turner, Victor, ed. *Celebration Studies in Festivity and Ritual.* Washington, D.C., Smithsonian Institution Press, 1982

_____. "Ritual Tribal and Catholic." *Worship 50* (6): 504-526

Van Gennep, Arnold. *The Rites of Passage.* Translated by Monika B. Vizedom and Gabrielle L. Caffee. Chicago University Press, 1960

Viorst, Judith. *Necessary Losses.* New York: Ballantine Books,1986

Author's email: T-Curley@Comcast.net

Made in the USA
Middletown, DE
30 May 2016